PERFECT PHRASES™

for

CONFLICT RESOLUTION

**Hundreds of Ready-to-Use Phrases
for Encouraging a More Productive
and Efficient Work Environment**

Lawrence Polsky and Antoine Gerschel

New York   Chicago   San Francisco   Lisbon   London   Madrid   Mexico City
Milan   New Delhi   San Juan   Seoul   Singapore   Sydney   Toronto

The *McGraw·Hill* Companies

6 7 8 9 10 11 12 13 14 15   QFR/QFR   1 9 8 7 6 5 4

ISBN   978-0-07-175616-7
MHID   0-07-175616-7

e-ISBN   978-0-07-176042-3
e-MHID   0-07-176042-3

Library of Congress Cataloging-in-Publication Data

Polsky, Lawrence.
    Perfect phrases for conflict resolution : hundreds of ready-to-use phrases for encouraging a more productive and efficient work environment / by Lawrence Polsky and Antoine Gerschel.
        p.   cm.
    ISBN-13: 978-0-07-175616-7 (alk. paper)
    ISBN-10: 0-07-175616-7 (alk. paper)
    1. Communication in management.   2. Interpersonal conflict.   3. Conflict management.   I. Gerschel, Antoine.   II. Title.

    HD30.3.P653   2011
    658.4'053—dc22   2011007335

McGraw-Hill books are available at special quantity discounts to use as premiums and sales promotions or for use in corporate training programs. To contact a representative, please e-mail us at bulksales@mcgraw-hill.com.

This book is printed on acid-free paper.

Contents

Acknowledgments

Anne Bruce, your continued support and enthusiasm for our work is an inspiration. Your energy and bighearted-ness continually amaze us. We are so grateful to have you as our guide, mentor, coach, friend, sister, and head cheerleader! This book would not exist without your support.

Thank you, Brian Foster, Mary Therese Church, and Lisa Stracks for your continued trust in our writing, for giving us just the right amount of direction to keep us on track, and for your editing. We have truly been in good hands! It has been a privilege to work with you and your team once again.

To our customers, thank you for so generously inviting us into your world! We learn daily from you and your organizational challenges. These experiences are the foundation of everything we do professionally and of many of the insights we share in this book.

Mark Kaplan, thank you for your continued insights into handling the most touchy of conflicts, particularly when long-held biases and discrimination are at play.

Thank you, Robin Famiglietti, Jim Higgins, Abha Mehta, Mediators without Borders, Mike Michalewicz, Barry Nobel, and Shelly

Bernstein, for the stories, questions, and examples that have encouraged us along the way.

To Teresa, Gretta, Zach, family, and friends, who are patient with me when I don't have the patience or skill to practice what we preach. Thank you for your generosity of spirit. Your love and support enable me to become a better person A special thank-you to Wilson Tilley—mentor, coach, and friend—who taught me the power of being open and honest in relationships. Everything I know about conflict resolution is rooted in your teaching. Your example proves irreplaceable to this day, both inside and outside of the workplace. Also to Bob Schachat, Nancy McManus, Steve Kleitzel, Lulinda Lloyd, Susan Mann, and all the others who frequented The Institute for Human Development in beautiful Charlemont. Without you, I could not have learned firsthand the ins and outs of bridging differences.

—Lawrence

To Noëmie, thank you for your partnership, your inspiration, and your patience. To Misha, Ron, and Giulia, I wish this book becomes a way for you to look at conflicts as an opportunity to grow personally and within the relationships you have. And, since you know me better than most readers, "Do what I say you should do, not what I do!"

—Antoine

CHAPTER

What Is Conflict Resolution?

There are two types of conflicts, particularly during any kind of change. The first we'll call direct conflict. This is when it is clear there is a difference of opinion, including:

- Your perception of the situation is at odds with another person's.
- Your point of view is at odds with someone else's.
- Your needs are at odds with another party's.

The second type of conflict involves situations where bad feelings develop over time and create a barrier to relationships and productivity. We call this latent conflict. This kind of conflict can result from a number of causes, such as one person not handling the initial situation well right away, a lack of skills on the part of one or more people in addressing the situation, or even the difficult personality of one or more people involved.

Why Do We Avoid Conflict?

At some point, everyone avoids conflicts at work, for reasons both good and bad. Think of a conflict you are currently avoiding. Perhaps the conflict has been lingering for a while, or maybe you think you can continue to do your work without resolving it. Whatever the case, something about this particular conflict is making you avoid getting it resolved. Some possible causes for avoiding resolution are that the conflict is:

- **Too risky.** You believe there is too much political risk to address it. A poorly handled conflict could result in fallout that will damage a project, a task, or even your career.
- **Unpleasant.** It is just hard.
- **Too personal.** You may think that the issue is not work related.
- **Difficult to control.** You do not have confidence you can control yourself. Or maybe the other party has a history of being explosive and you think you don't have the skills to manage the situation.

And as you may have experienced yourself, the tendency to avoid conflict is particularly high when dealing with latent conflicts. Direct conflicts easily burst into the open and require a solution, whether we like it or not.

These reasons for avoidance are all real and valid, as are many others. This book will help you overcome these and other obstacles and find an approach that will enable you to address conflict productively and professionally.

Can Conflict Be Resolved?

We have yet to run across an organization where all conflict is resolved. Conflict ebbs and flows in relationships in organizations. In fact, if we saw no conflict during change in an organization (and as we all know they are continuously changing!), we would suspect the organization to be dying or already dead! The emotional exchange of ideas and perceptions is a natural part of people working together.

Employees at all levels must continue working even when conflicts and ambiguities exist. Of course, there are some work conflict situations that can be addressed through a short dialogue to clear up misunderstandings. Many others, however, take more work. They require more energy, a willingness to revisit the issue, and a personal commitment to working things out in the long term.

If you are looking at resolution as all parties being completely happy with the outcome, then resolution is not attainable in most situations. Often, one person will be happy and another not. Partnerships may not be even; there may be a clear hierarchy between, for example, boss and subordinate or customer and supplier and the party in power just decides. Even if there is a more balanced partnership, it can take a lot of effort and time to create a "win/win." We don't always have the energy and time to approach it this way. Other times a conflict—particularly latent conflicts—drags on, sometimes even a long time. We hope it dissipates by itself—and sometimes it does, either because the situation has changed (again), key players change, or it may just become less important due to new priorities or a different mood (different emotions) of the main parties.

Rules of Engagement

What does it take to successfully resolve conflict?

1. Conflict Resolution Is Not for the Faint of Heart

As a first step in approaching conflict resolution, look honestly at yourself to see whether you have what it takes to address conflict. Attributes of a good conflict handler include:

■ **Courage.** Conflict always involves potential misinterpretation and hurt feelings. It takes courage to walk calmly and deliberately through the ambiguity and try to resolve it.

■ **Balancing your interests with the interests of others.** Ultimately, you must care about the other person and her or her point of view to resolve conflict. If you focus too much on yourself, you are being inflexible. Too much focus on the other party, on the other hand, means you overlook your own needs. It takes a balanced view.

■ **Thinking on your feet.** Being prepared is important. However, don't expect to have your conflict resolution plan all worked out and be able to stick with it. Humans are unpredictable, even the ones we know the best, so plan on adjusting your plan.

■ **Letting go of the "resolution."** To be effective in conflict, one must adopt the mind-set of living in the state of ambiguity. Many times, you will have to live with an ongoing subtext of disagreement until sometime in the future when the issue may be resolved. Then again, it may never be resolved, or it may be resolved to the satisfaction of the other person but not you. The bottom line is that you must accept that conflict will always exist, while a completely satisfying resolution may not.

2. Know When to Give in and When to Hold Your Ground

A simple way to avoid unnecessary conflict and to only fight for your point of view when necessary is to think about how much interest you have in the outcome of a particular conflict compared to how much interest the other party has. Using these two dimensions, you can easily decide how to approach the conflict:

- **Low interest to you, low interest to the other party:** Forget it. This is not worth debating.

- **Low interest to you, high interest to the other party:** Give in. Why turn it into a fight if you don't really care about it?

- **High interest to you, low interest to the other party:** Advocate. In situations where the outcome affects you more than the other person or people, be strong and advocate your position.

- **High interest to you, high interest to the other party:** Collaborate. The only way to come up with a productive solution is for both parties to work together. These are also the situations that can become the most contentious because both parties care so much about the results.

3. Balance Cooperation and Advocacy

The central art of handling conflict is balancing being cooperative while at the same time advocating for your point of view.

How direct should you be? If you are too passive, you will focus too much on making the other party happy at your expense or at the expense of the business issue. If you are too aggressive, you wind up focusing more on getting your way than on the other party's feelings and point of view. When you are aggressive, you might also be blaming the other person for the problem. The challenge is to find the middle ground: being assertive. This means to encourage and support the other person's openness while advocating your point of view. It means taking both your and the other person's thoughts, feelings, and wants into account.

These phrases will help you know which part of the spectrum you are on:

Passive

- Whatever you do is OK with me.
- It doesn't matter.
- Whatever.

Aggressive

- You always _____.
- You never _____.
- What is the matter with you?

Assertive

■ I hear you saying that _____. However, what I want/need is _____. The reason(s) I need this is/are _____. Does that make sense? Let's see if we can come up with a mutually workable solution.

■ I understand that you are having a problem with _____. I would like to make a request. The next time this happens, could we _____?

■ This doesn't seem to be working for either of us. It is not working for me because _____. What would work better for me is _____. Would that work for you?

4. Be Direct and Avoid Triangulation

Talk to the person with whom you have the conflict. While you may decide to speak to someone who is not involved for advice on how to handle a situation, asking that person to take sides or intervene on your behalf only creates more interpersonal problems. Such an action erodes trust and reduces the chance of future issues being resolved. (See the section on cultural aspects later in this chapter for further discussion.)

5. Reduce Static

What we call static is anything within a person or an environment that interferes with clear communication. It is the same concept as the static on the radio when you try to tune in to a station and can't get good reception. The resulting noise is a distraction from the song you want to hear.

Static can be in our environment as well as in our head. Some common examples of static are:

■ Background noise

■ Physical distractions—pain, hunger, or fatigue

■ Jumping to solutions—moving too quickly to solve an issue, without considering the whole situation, can cause disruption

■ Asking too many questions—if you are asking questions all the time and interrupting the talker, you may be overtaking the conversation

■ Interruptions—other people, walking in from outside, can be static. Find out what they are looking for. Is it an emergency? Do they want advice? Do they just want someone to talk to? Depending on the situation, you should ask for a meeting at a more appropriate time.

■ Your own mind—you can think much faster than you can speak! Your mind has extra bandwidth and naturally wanders away. So what can you do to help with that extra bandwidth? Make your conversation more interactive. Pause. Ask for your listener's input. Check whether he or she has any questions.

When discussing contentious issues, set up a time and place when you and your colleague can give the discussion your full attention. This will let both of you focus your mind and energy on the conversation.

Phases of Conflict

All of the phrases in this book follow a four-step process to handle conflict:

1. Understand the issue
2. Set a vision
3. Explore alternatives
4. Agree on action

Following this simple structure increases your success in conflict situations. With that said, it is hard to always follow it perfectly. It is meant as a guideline to address the key aspects of conflict situations.

Each of these four steps is further outlined below:

Understand the Issue

Framing the beginning of the conversation as an opportunity to understand the issue, rather than as a fight or argument, will make it easier to begin the resolution process. Here are the key elements of this step:

■ **Ask for a meeting:** Before speaking with the person with whom you have a conflict, ask for a meeting. It is always best if you and your colleague can focus on the issue without being disturbed. You may also want to prepare so you can handle the meeting effectively.

You may not want to disclose any of the details of the topic of conversation in an e-mail or a phone call when setting up a meeting. Once you bring up the issue, the conversation starts. If both of you are not in a place or space to fully discuss it, the conversation can backfire because neither of you can do justice to the complexity and emotions of the topic.

Instead, try saying something like "I would like to meet with you to discuss an important issue." If the other person asks you what that topic is, it is better to say something along the lines of "It would be best to discuss it when we can both focus on it." This communicates that the topic is not quick, that it is important, and that it could be complicated and emotional, which helps ensure he or she sets up a time and place for such a conversation. In addition, he or she will be curious and come ready to listen.

Here is an example:

Employee: "Mary, I'd like to schedule a meeting with you to discuss an important issue."

Boss: "What is it?"

Employee: "I'd rather talk about it when we both have time to talk with our full attention. When would you have thirty minutes?"

Boss: "I need to know what it is so I can prepare."

Employee: "I understand that. However, if I open the conversation now it will just complicate things. Are you willing to trust me and we can take all the time we need at the meeting?"

When the meeting begins, you will need to raise the issue. You will notice in our phrases we begin with raising the issue, the first part of any conflict resolution, which is often the hardest.

■ **Open discussion:** It helps to find a neutral or positive way to open the discussion such as talking about other things, business or personal.

■ **Share specifics:** Make sure that you come to the discussion prepared. Have specific examples and cases in mind so you can help make the conversation concrete and prevent it from escalating into blaming and accusations.

Raise the issue by being as specific as possible. Mention the specific situation(s) or events(s) that upset you. If you can identify behaviors, such as what the other person did or did not say or do, that is particularly helpful. This will help focus the conversation rather than the other person perceiving you as attacking him or her.

■ **Discuss impact:** If possible, explain the impact the event had on you, the team, other people, the business, or customers. Again, this will help the other person understand that you are not raising this issue just to be difficult.

■ **Listen:** A key part of understanding the issue is to understand the other person's point of view. Ask questions. Be curious. Follow the guidelines later in this chapter on listening. This will go a long way toward building understanding and ultimately to resolving the conflict.

Set a Vision

Before you decide to address a conflict, you need to be very clear about what your objectives are in addressing it. Do you want to:

■ Improve a relationship?

■ Resolve a business issue?

- Assure better service quality or deliver best customer service?
- Promote yourself?
- Make future life at work easier?
- Get compliance with the process you are in charge of?

Articulating a vision for the future, after you have explored the issue, will help both parties move beyond the past and into a more positive frame of mind.

Explore Alternatives

Once the vision is out on the table, both parties can openly discuss how to get there. The phrases at this stage are either questions to get the other person's ideas on how to rectify the situation or your suggestions on how to do the same:

- How are you going to do it?
- How can I help?
- What ideas do you have to prevent this in the future?
- What could you do to make sure this doesn't happen again?
- I'll need a little time to process this before we talk some more.
- In the future could you include me on _____ before taking action?
- For the next project, let's meet when we start and clearly define roles, responsibilities, and decision-making process.

■ I might need to talk to _____ if we cannot work this out.

Use these types of questions or suggestions—or both—as your situation warrants.

Agree on Action

If you get this far, you are likely to get to agreement. The only exception would be if the two of you cannot agree on how to fix the problem. If that is the case, you may want to ask for a chance to think it over and meet again. Or you may need to inform him or her of your intention to escalate the issue. Whatever the case, make sure to end with being clear about who is going to do what.

Handling Emotions

The facts or figures are often not the problem in conflict; the emotions are. Depending on the personalities, situations, power-differentials, and skills of each party, conflict creates a wide range of personal emotional reactions.

Take the situation of a difference of opinion with your manager about your performance. The facts may be unclear as to whether you have met your manager's expectations. Expectations are subjective and may not have been outlined specifically. In addition, your manager has more organizational power than you. Especially if it is a situation where money and career advancement are at stake, the emotions can begin to ratchet up.

Fear, anxiety, and stress can build and create a barrier to clear communication. Blaming, avoidance, and/or arguing often ensue. The approaches in this book are meant to reduce emotions and create clarity and understanding.

Strategies for Handling Negative Emotions

There are several approaches you can use to reduce the negative emotions in yourself and others during conflict. The following are some ideas and phrases you can use:

- Sit at the same side of the table. This reduces the psychological barrier of the table and opens up the communication.

- Delay: "Let's talk about it later when we have more time to think it through."

- Lower expectations: "I know you won't like this but I think we need to talk about it anyway."

- Start with the positive: "You are very good at _____ however, _____."

- Break the tension by being relaxed and personal: "I am so glad we are talking about this." "You are really someone I trust to work this through with."

- Include commonalities and points of agreements as you're discussing the differences: "You are right we do need to work on _____. It is also getting clear from this conversation that we are doing pretty well with _____."

- Acknowledge the other person's difficulty: "I see that this is a challenge for you." "I hear that you are having a hard time with _____."

- Take responsibility for your part in the problem: "I see now how I am contributing to this by doing _____."

- Take responsibility for solving the problem: "Next time I _____."

- Apologize, if necessary: "I am so sorry I create this problem." "I apologize for inadvertently creating such reactions."

Counterproductive Conflict Beliefs

What comes first, thoughts or feelings? The research on emotional intelligence shows that thoughts come first. Imagine how it feels when someone you don't like walks into your office; you have a feeling of dread or stress. If you track back to what you were thinking when he or she walked in, you will realize that you had a negative thought, such as "Oh no," or "I don't want to deal with this right now."

Our thoughts can be our own worst enemy during conflict. Some thoughts/beliefs that we have found to interfere with resolving conflict include:

- "It may resolve itself"—this creates a delay in resolving the issue and may even build a bigger problem.

- "It is not important enough"—this thought minimizes the person and the issue, which may come back to haunt you.

- "He or she will never understand"—this becomes a self-fulfilling prophecy.

- "It is useless"—this is another self-fulfilling prophecy.

- "It's not me, it is my boss's job to handle this"—this puts the responsibility on someone else's shoulders.

- "We can't have that conversation here"—having that conversation is just plain hard work and no one wants to do it.

Listening

Part of the frustration in any conflict comes from feeling like the other person doesn't understand. He or she is not listening.

Lack of listening by either side escalates conflict. Before you tell the other person you disagree or make your point yet again, try listening to him or her. Even a small bit of listening will go a long way to increase understanding and reduce conflict.

Should you think listening is for those who are not strong enough to take charge, take a cue from Jim Higgins, a former police officer. Jim worked for thirteen years in enforcement on the streets in New York, dealing with drug dealers, prostitutes, gambling, and domestic disputes across cultures and neighborhoods.

We had the privilege of interviewing him about the secret to effective policing and de-escalating conflict. Is it force? Is it psychology? Is it fear?

Surprisingly, Jim said that none of those were the answer. Whether dealing with an angry tenant or a psychotic claiming his mother is a Russian spy, he says the secret is to "Listen. Mirror what people are saying. Try from the beginning to be understanding and kind. It calms people down. Once you start to act like a tough guy, you can't go back and be understanding—it is too late."

So how can you do this?

First, focus on the other person. In today's busy world of a hundred e-mails a day, multiple work projects, and constant pressure, everyone is stressed. Help yourself focus by looking at the other person, taking notes about the conversation, turning away from the computer, shutting off the monitor, closing e-mail. Focus your attention on him or her, not on yourself.

Remember that there are always multiple levels of communication going on—the actual words, the tone of voice, and body language. Words are easiest, but even then you can be misled. Voice tone is not so much up for interpretation, but it is still important. For example, "Yeah, right" said in an agreeable tone is far different than "Yeah, right" said in a sarcastic tone. The words are the same, but the change of tone makes a big difference.

The same is true for many body postures, which can have multiple meanings. A good thing to keep in mind is the change of a body posture. For example, if we are talking and, in the middle of the conversation, I cross my arms, that posture change means something has probably changed in my perception of the conversation.

Most important, explore the other person's point of view. What is he or she talking about? Why are his or her beliefs what they are? Ask sincere questions to gain understanding so that you will be able to:

- Get more information on his or her point of view
- Communicate you care about how he or she sees things
- Move from the emotion-laden part of your brain to the rational side

By asking questions, you can explore his or her point of view:

- Why do you think that?
- What makes you feel that way?

- What happened to give you that impression?
- What did I say that led you to that conclusion?

You can also paraphrase what you heard to make sure you understand the other person's point of view correctly. Such phrases as the following will help you mirror his or her words well:

- It sounds like you are saying . . .
- Do you mean . . .
- Let me make sure I understand you. You said . . .

Culture and Conflict

Do you work in a culture in which people address conflicts or one in which people avoid conflicts? How do you know?

For starters, consider your meetings. Are they animated, engaged, full of constructive dialogue? Do they include conflicting point of views and discussions about them? In this case, you may be in a culture that is open to conflict.

If your meetings are boring and usually just include the presentation facts, it may mean that the participants of the meeting have little in common and no overlapping responsibilities; however, often it is an indication for conflict avoidance. Conflict-avoidance cultures have destroyed more value than any other single business behavior! Look at it this way: To have a healthy discourse and discuss new and opposing ideas is a key ingredient to innovation, business process improvements, and personal development. On the other side, if you don't dare to bring up thought-provoking ideas, voice concern, or break with "common wisdom," you, your department, and your company will continue to dwell in the "same old, same old." Problems may be ignored until they blow up with a big bang. Often it is too late by then.

Issues of Power

Managing conflict is difficult. When you add in important aspects of diversity, such as race, gender, sexual orientation, age, and culture, it can get even more complicated.

When two people have many similarities, even if the conflict is strong, there is a good possibility of resolving the conflict successfully. The more differences there are between the two parties, the more complicated resolution gets.

Amounts of organizational power are based on the groups people belong to. A simple example is level in the hierarchy. You have likely been supervised by someone and know how careful you need to be when differences of opinions or strong feelings occur. You might even have had the experience of not raising an important issue due to a concern that your manager wouldn't understand you or would even punish you in some way for raising the issue. This is because your boss has more power than you.

This may also be the case if you are from a different culture or ethnic group or even sexual orientation than most people in the organization. When engaging the conflict, you might not want to "rock the boat," especially if you are trying to fit in to a group while being the only person like yourself.

How Do We Reduce Power Differences?

Many executives report they wish they would get more pushback from their staff. They would like to be challenged and disagreed with. They purport to have "open door policies" and believe they are creating open climates where disagreements can be aired freely. Yet very few staff take them up on the offer. These leaders are either unaware of or unable to change the dynamic.

Having power can be blinding. Thus the challenge in managing conflict across differences is most significant when you are in the more dominant powerful position. The more power you have (vis-à-vis group memberships), the more you need to exhibit the following behaviors:

■ **Be aware of power differences.** In any conflict situation, look at the group membership differences in the people involved. Consider race, culture, gender, age, sexual orientation, organizational level, and any other difference that has resonance within the organization. Might they be hesitant to speak up or to give in? Might they feel superior and listen less? For example, women may have to walk a fine line when presenting a different opinion—they could be concerned about being perceived as not a team player or as too pushy. Men can be blunt and direct; while such behavior might be uncomfortable, it would be perceived as being "really upset" or regarding something "really important" rather than being pushy.

■ **Consider the impact of bias.** Ask yourself what biases you might hold that will affect your behavior. For example, is it OK when a man pushes back but not when a woman does? Do you expect your employees to follow what you say just because you are the boss? Then consider how these biases might impact the outcome of the conflict.

■ **Work hard to build relationships.** Build relationships across differences by being genuinely interested in people who are different from you. Seek them out and inquire about their lives, perspectives, and experiences. Take extra time to explore their point of view. Building strong relationships will make it easier to discuss tough issues when they come up.

CHAPTER 2

Perfect Phrases for Resolving Conflict with Your Boss

Your boss is your most important customer. If that seems odd, think of it this way. He or she is paying you, giving you opportunities, and teaching you.

Keep in mind that you would do well to treat your manager as you would your most important customer. You want to please him or her and do everything you can to accommodate his or her needs. Like customers, supervisors make requests and make you do things that create work and often are difficult. You do them because he or she is your lifeblood. If you can't serve your supervisor, he or she will find someone else to meet his or her needs. Remember, too, that your boss is not and will never be perfect. Sometimes you have to accept his or her imperfections, just as he or she tolerates yours.

There are times, however, when customers and bosses may display a behavior that seriously impacts you or your team's productivity. You know that if it is not addressed, you run the risk of failure, which would be in nobody's interest. This is when you may have one of the conversations that this chapter deals with.

As with anyone in conflict, know your boss. Some bosses are direct and appreciate straight dealings. They want direct dialogue. Others are more sensitive to what can be perceived as criticism. Our phrases are written for the second, more delicate kinds of situations. If you have a boss who is more direct, you can skip some of the wording and transitions and get right to it.

Perfect Phrases for Resolving Performance Issues

The following are some helpful phrases for when you receive feedback from your boss that your performance is lower than you believe it is:

→ Thank you for taking the time to meet with me.

→ It is really important for me to . . .

  → do a good job.

  → have you see the value of my work.

  → be valued on the team.

  → be in sync with you.

  → create results.

→ Based on our conversation earlier about my performance, I want to make sure . . .

  → I don't jump to conclusions.

  → you understand my point of view.

  → you hear what I am saying.

  → I understand your point of view.

→ It seems as if you think . . .

  → my report didn't meet your expectations.

  → my handling of customer X was inadequate.

  → I didn't take enough leadership in the last project meeting.

> - → I wasn't responsive to your new ideas.
> - → I haven't learned the new software fast enough.

- → I appreciate your "yes!" This helps me to know that I have understood what you are telling me.
- → Thank you for your candor!
- → Could you remember any specific examples you'd be willing to share with me?
- → Can you tell me . . .
  - → specifically what was wrong with my report?
  - → more specifically what I did inappropriately when handling the customer?
  - → specifically what you wanted me to do in the meeting?
  - → what reaction I displayed that led to your conclusion that I am not responsive to your new idea?
  - → what features of the software you think I don't know that I should by now?
- → Thank you for your honesty and feedback. Can I have some time to think this over and schedule a meeting to continue the conversation?
- → I hear what you are saying and very much respect your point of view. However, . . .
  - → I see it a little differently.
  - → I respectfully disagree.
  - → that is not how I see it.

→ When I wrote the report, I used the model you approved last time. I assumed this was still a valid approach. I am surprised by this change in format. I need clarity from you on how you would like the report going forward. Can we take a few minutes and get that defined right now?

→ I made my decision based on _____. At the time, given what I knew, it seemed like the right decision. It seems like you are holding me to an unreachable standard. We need to come up with a way in the future to get in agreement ahead of time.

→ What I have observed in those meetings is that whenever there is a pause, you like to chime in and take the lead of the conversation. Since you are my boss, I feel like I should follow your lead. I am happy about what you are saying. I am very motivated to be the leader in those meetings. In the future, I would love it if you could either give me a minute to jump in first or ask me "what do you think?" before taking the lead.

Perfect Phrases for Telling Your Boss You Have Too Many High Priorities

➜ May I ask you for a meeting? Would _____ at _____ work for you?

➜ I know we are under a lot of pressure right now to get results. However, . . .

   ➜ I am a bit confused about what is important.

   ➜ I am not sure what are my top priorities.

   ➜ I need some clarity on my priorities.

   ➜ there seems to be a conflict in priorities.

   ➜ everything seems like it is the top priority.

➜ For example, . . .

   ➜ both of the new report designs need to be done by next week.

   ➜ I was just called in for this new project kickoff meeting while I am consumed by _____.

   ➜ I have _____ number of proposals to write in the next forty-eight hours.

   ➜ the marketing team is telling me that product X takes priority.

   ➜ R&D has asked me to do this additional investigation of _____.

→ Can you tell me . . .

  → what is the ranking of importance?

  → what you see as the most important?

  → how I could sort this out?

  → if there is anyone who can help me with this?

→ Thank you for your time! I'd like to summarize our agreement as me focusing on _____ first, then addressing _____. Only if there is any extra time do I worry about _____.

→ Do you agree?

→ May I send you an e-mail confirming this understanding?

Perfect Phrases for When There Aren't Enough Resources

➜ Thank you for taking the time to meet with me.

➜ I know times are tight now and we have to do more with less.

➜ You have said that we need to be more creative with the resources we have.

➜ I have been around long enough to know that there is never enough time/money/people here.

➜ However, . . .

   ➜ it seems like I keep getting more and more on my plate with no additional help.

   ➜ the list of objectives keeps growing while the resources are shrinking.

   ➜ there isn't enough time in the day anymore.

   ➜ everyone is pressing me to create more results.

   ➜ I cannot be all things to all people.

   ➜ it seems like there is unrealistic planning going on.

➜ Specifically, . . .

   ➜ I am working sixty hours a week and there is no end in sight.

   ➜ I worked all weekend to prepare for the project meeting—and this was not the first time.

→ Pauline gave me another project to work on, on top of everything else.

→ the deadline for the system rollout was moved up a month and we lost two people on the implementation team.

Follow-up phrases:

→ Do you have any suggestions?

→ Do you have any creative ideas?

Perfect Phrases for Unfair Treatment

➔ I have something I need to discuss with you. It's very important.

➔ When would you have time for me?

➔ You want to know what it is about? I'd rather take the time to explain it to you in detail when we meet. You do not need to prepare for it. For the time being, thank you for blocking out the time!

➔ Thank you for taking the time to meet with me—even without knowing what we are going to talk about.

➔ I have asked you to meet because I'm worried. I need to clarify the situation to make sure I understand what is going on and I'm not coming to any wrong conclusions.

➔ I have observed that everybody else in the department seems to . . .

  ➔ have gotten a raise.

  ➔ have gotten a special project assignment.

  ➔ be going out for long lunches.

  ➔ be attending conferences.

➔ Bringing up the topic is very difficult for me. I know that this may not have been done intentionally.

➔ However, can you see how this could be very upsetting?

➔ May I give you an example so you can better understand?

→ I don't want to mention any names, but I know for a fact that quite a few of our group have received considerable pay raises.

→ I'm referring to (name of person)'s assignment to _____. I respect him or her a lot and think he or she deserved this assignment. At the same time, I'm really disappointed since I had been waiting for such an opportunity for a long time, and we had talked about it.

→ (Names of people) started the tradition of meeting for lunch at Lucie's. By the time they are back, two hours may have easily gone by. I'm bringing it up because I have to cover the phone while they are away and am getting dragged into customer-service conversations I normally would not be part of.

→ (Name of people) attended _____. I would also have liked to go there but was not chosen.

Perfect Phrases for Advocating a Change Your Boss Thinks Is Not Necessary

➜ I'd like to talk to you about this new initiative. It may not be your top priority but it would be helpful to schedule some time to discuss the way I should react to requests coming up. I need your advice.

➜ What this initiative is trying to achieve is _____.

➜ There is a natural back-and-forth between you and your team about how to improve.

➜ I understand you need to be convinced before investing any time and money.

➜ I have backed down too easily in the past or taken the "no" as a personal rejection. This is why this conversation is very important.

➜ I would like to explore your point of view a little further.

➜ Why do you think that . . .

   ➜ more advertising is not necessary?

   ➜ we don't need any more people?

   ➜ I shouldn't go to this conference?

   ➜ our current strategy is working?

   ➜ this new process will not work?

   ➜ we do not have the time to expand the product offering to new markets?

→ To make sure I understand what you are saying, let me try it with my own words. Are you saying . . .

> → you want to use the marketing money for other initiatives?
>
> → the headcount may be going to a different project or department?
>
> → I may be allowed to go to this conference next year, but there are far too many other burning priorities now to allow me to leave?
>
> → we are to abandon the strategy I have been suggesting and move to a new one?
>
> → you don't like my suggestion or that you think it is the wrong timing?
>
> → we are not going to expand our product offering because we have been burned in the past?

→ What would it take to change your mind?

→ If we knew it would be successful, would we do it?

→ I remember distinct success stories from the past. Do you remember when we _____?

→ I'd like to recap the relevant aspects of our business case.

> → The reason I make this suggestion is _____. What are the reasons behind what you are suggesting?
>
> → The top three benefits of this approach are _____.

➜ Things will improve if we do this
because _____.

➜ The cost of not doing anything is _____.

➜ So I have your support?

➜ Do you want me to further detail aspect X of my plan?

➜ I will get back to you by _____.

➜ With your approval, I'll reach out to _____ and get his or her opinion.

➜ There is also a Plan B. Would you like me to scope out more details of this plan?

➜ It appears that there is an insurmountable problem around _____. We should break it apart and analyze each aspect of it and how we could mitigate its impact. Would you agree?

Perfect Phrases for an Emergency Meeting with Your Boss

→ I am trying to understand the urgency of this conversation. . . .

  → Can you please explain to me what is going on and why you need me in this meeting?

  → What is happening?

  → What is the goal of this meeting?

  → You think I am the best person or the only available person?

→ I understand that _____.

→ I was planning to leave in a few minutes because _____. Let's look at a couple of quick options:

  → Is there a way we could move the part that I'm involved with to the beginning of the meeting so I could leave as soon as I have answered those questions?

  → I'd be happy to call in while I'm in the car.

  → My collaborator _____ knows as much of this issue as I do. Would you mind if he or she joined?

  → Is there any way we could reschedule this item to the next meeting when I can block out the time to participate?

→ OK, so we are meeting tomorrow at _____ to discuss.

→ Thank you very much for your consideration!

Perfect Phrases for Conflict with Another Superior

→ We seem to have a clear disagreement in this matter.

  → I have not spoken to my boss about it yet.

  → Do you think I should first speak to my supervisor before we speak?

  → Would you go to a superior who wasn't your boss and talk to him or her directly?

→ I suggest we schedule a meeting to go through this issue and eliminate any misunderstandings. In the meantime, I will touch base with my boss to make sure I properly understand his or her priorities beforehand. Or would you rather have the three of us meet together?

→ Good, I am confirming that we are meeting on _____ at _____ in your office.

→ Please allow me to start this meeting by telling you how much I enjoy our collaboration.

  → You have been a coach and mentor of mine.

  → I would not be where I am without you.

  → I have very fond memories of the _____ project, which we pulled off together.

  → I have very high respect for your experience and your leadership.

→ Everybody in our company admires you, and it's a privilege to have the opportunity to work with you on this project.

→ It makes it all the more important for me to resolve a potential difference of opinions we may have.

→ You are the _____, and you are a key member of the leadership here. I want you to be satisfied with me and my work. This is why I'm checking in with you to know whether you are OK with what I am doing and the contribution I am making to the company.

→ If I understand you right, you are saying that _____. Is that correct?

→ Do you have some advice for me? You have been here a long time so I'm interested to hear what you have to say.

Perfect Phrases for Dealing with a Micromanaging Boss

Micromanagers do what they do to control. It may be because they are inexperienced managers or because they think you are not capable of doing it on your own. They also may not want to spend the time to teach you how to do it as well as they do. In any case, they want to guarantee success. Keep all this in mind while considering having and preparing for this discussion.

→ I have asked for this meeting and thank you for taking the time to meet with me.

→ The topic I would like to discuss is not an easy one.

→ The conversation is difficult for me.

→ I know you are my boss, and first and foremost I want to do anything I can to support you and our success in the best way I can.

→ I know that my job is critical to our department's/this project's/our product's success.

→ I want to do the best job possible.

→ I know you have a lot of experience in this job/position/function.

→ I know you want to help me succeed.

→ I value your guidance.

→ You sometimes know things about the situation that I don't.

→ There is this one thing, which has been a challenge for me, that I thought you may want to know.

→ I also want to ask your advice about how to overcome it.

→ Let me share a few examples to make it clear.

→ Don't get me wrong. While many of these examples may seem small, they are just a few to illustrate the issue.

→ We recently prepared slides for _____ meeting. You probably noticed that we created twelve versions. It went as far as making last-minute changes as we walked into the meeting. I appreciated your input and ideas with each change.

→ However, this reduced my productivity in the meeting because . . .

    → it ratcheted up my stress level/reduced my confidence/created a fear of not being in sync with you.

    → I wanted to focus on meeting the customer's needs but I was also worried that you were going to change your mind in the middle and I wouldn't be able to meet your needs, too.

→ Every week, I need to complete the _____ report, which documents my _____ activities. At least once a day, you also send me e-mails asking me details about my weekly calendar. Just yesterday I replied to such an e-mail and you responded by questioning the choices I was making about how I block out my time. I understand your need to ensure I am being productive and to make sure I am working on the right priorities. However, . . .

→ this makes it hard to stay focused on getting my work done.

→ it feels like I am spending a lot of time justifying my activities rather than producing.

→ it feels like an imbalance of focus on quantity versus quality.

→ Do you remember that instance?

→ What is your point of view on that?

→ What do you think?

→ So it seems like we agree that _____.

→ I just want to check that I understand our priorities. Our goal is _____.

→ Can we agree the next time we do slides we . . .

→ create a maximum of _____ revisions?

→ freeze the version _____ day/hours(s) before the meeting?

→ Could we meet once a week so I can highlight the priorities for the coming week and we can come to an agreement?

Perfect Phrases for When a Manager Minimizes Your Contributions

→ Thank you for agreeing to speak with me today.

→ This is a difficult issue to raise.

→ Your task orientation is very helpful. It makes us very productive. I am proud to be working on our team.

→ Please don't take this the wrong way. It is clear from the assignments I have been getting that you believe I am a key team member.

→ Don't get me wrong, I love my work here, but there is one thing that may get in the way of my productivity.

→ I may be overly sensitive, but it would be really nice if you could pause and tell me what is being done well.

→ It would be very helpful for me to know what I am doing right so that I can make sure I keep doing that.

→ Your feedback helps me be better at my job. However, when you harp on a minor error, it is very discouraging and makes me question if I am doing anything right.

→ I have observed that my team's contributions are never mentioned at the higher level meetings.

→ I would love it if we could walk through my main projects and define your expectations for success.

Perfect Phrases for a Manager Who Doesn't Listen to Your Ideas

➔ We have successfully worked for _____. I feel comfortable and privileged to have you as my boss.

➔ This is why I am going to share something with you that is difficult to express.

➔ It seems like that when I present an idea, you are not listening.

➔ I am not sure if you heard me correctly at our meeting on _____. What I meant was _____.

➔ This is not the first time you misunderstood my ideas. Another occasion was regarding _____ on _____.

➔ I am interested in your advice. I am wondering if there is a way I can present my ideas more clearly?

➔ What suggestions do you have for me about advocating my point of view?

➔ My objective is not that you do what I suggest, but that at least I get a sense that you heard it and that I hear any feedback as to why it is not a workable idea.

➔ Your direct comments will help me learn and be able to contribute more productively in the future.

➔ Would it be helpful if . . .

    ➔ I followed up my verbal suggestions with an e-mail detailing my thought process?

→ I made a brief suggestion and asked for your immediate comments?

→ set up a separate meeting with you when I have new ideas?

→ Thank you for your help.

→ I appreciate your point of view.

→ Going forward I will _____.

→ I am confident this will help us be more productive in the future.

Perfect Phrases for a Manager Who Is Not Available

→ I understand you are very busy.

→ I admire how much you get done in a workday.

→ I appreciate you giving me the freedom to make my own decisions and follow my own trail.

→ The last thing I want is to have a micromanager for my boss.

→ On the other hand, if I can check in with you more regularly, I think we can be even more . . .

  → productive.

  → responsive.

  → effective.

  → accurate.

  → innovative.

  → energized.

  → aligned.

→ I wanted to talk to you about scheduling time to get help with issues.

→ Sometimes I need your input and don't know how to reach you.

→ For instance, when I was working on _____ yesterday with _____, we would have been able to negotiate an even better solution if we had been able to strategize for fifteen minutes ahead of time.

→ When I was talking to customer X, I don't think I would have made the commitment I made if I had known what you told me after the phone call.

→ Had I known that the new position opened for _____, I would have told you about _____, who is an outstanding professional and would have been a perfect fit for that job.

→ If I had known the agenda of _____ meeting, I could have . . .

   → attended to address the problem with _____.

   → prepared by researching _____.

   → asked _____ to attend.

   → prevented the decision about _____, which is not helping our operations.

→ Can we agree on a process to connect each week to review hot topics?

→ What would be a good time for a daily check-in call to get help if I need it?

Perfect Phrases for a Manager Who Lashes Out

→ I respect your expertise and knowledge of our business.

→ You have excellent judgment of what will work.

→ Like you, I am very interested in getting the best ideas implemented.

→ I understand the pressure to get the job done here is very high.

→ I am not one to shy away from direct debate.

→ I don't want to misinterpret your behavior.

→ Sometimes it seems that in the pursuit of success, we end up disregarding each other's feelings.

→ I am noticing you are very emotional about this topic. Is that right?

→ Can you tell me a little more about why this issue is so important to you?

→ Maybe it would be best to take a short break and come back to this when we have more time.

→ It is really demotivating and interfering with my productivity when you . . .

  → talk in that demeaning tone.

  → roll your eyes.

  → shoot out another idea before discussing the ones on the table.

→ I know you are not acting this way on purpose; however, it is really getting in the way.

→ I have noticed that you don't speak this way all the time. Is there something about my approach/timing/wording that creates this reaction?

→ How can we come up with a way to critique ideas and not people?

→ This behavior is not acceptable. I want it to stop. I will be reporting this to HR.

Perfect Phrases for Not Being Included

→ I am not sure how to bring this up, but I was very disappointed to discover that the decision about _____ was made without my input.

→ I know there are a lot of moving parts on this initiative. However, you may not have realized that the decision about _____ affects me and my team.

→ This is very frustrating because . . .

    → I am very committed to _____.

    → I am working above and beyond on this project and am highly qualified to contribute to this decision process.

    → my team and I will have to implement this decision.

    → our team will bear the brunt of the decision.

➜ We have a history in this company of other decisions being made excluding key stakeholders. This has led to less than satisfactory results, to put it mildly. For example, _____.

➜ My plate is full. I have a lot to do, and the last thing I want is more. However, I must raise the flag here because . . .

  ➜ this decision falls squarely in my area. There are very few people in the organization who know as much about this as I do.

  ➜ the _____ point of view is excluded. This leads to not having a holistic view and, in turn, to potentially poor decisions.

  ➜ this is not about me personally but about the quality of the decision.

  ➜ based on my understanding of my job description, I should have been included.

➜ This gives me the impression that you don't trust . . .

  ➜ me.

  ➜ my point of view.

  ➜ my experience.

  ➜ our team.

➜ What happened?

➜ Did I miss something?

➜ What is your take on it?

➜ How can I get inserted into the process?

➜ What can we do next time to avoid this?

Perfect Phrases for When Your Manager Does Not Support Your Advancement

→ I have a very important topic to discuss with you. Can we schedule some time?

→ I want to talk about my career development. I hope we can get about an hour of uninterrupted time. When can we meet?

→ I very much appreciate the time I have had at our company since _____ and the opportunities I have had to grow.

→ I value our working relationship. It is a big part of my job satisfaction.

→ I have enjoyed my time here and have learned a lot.

→ I am driven by having opportunities to . . .

  → grow my skills.

  → move up in the organization.

  → take on more complex projects.

  → earn more money.

  → learn about other areas of the organization.

  → partner with internal thought leaders.

  → get exposure to senior management.

→ However, . . .

  → I was passed over for a recent promotion.

  → when the new project came up, it was assigned to someone else.

- → I have yet to be invited to a _____ meeting.
- → I have not gone to an industry conference since _____.
- → I have not received a raise since _____.
- → I am not included in the strategic meetings and projects.
- → I was not involved in the decision regarding _____.

→ Please tell me how you see it.

→ Is this different than your experience?

→ What can I do differently?

→ Is there something I don't know that would help me for future opportunities?

→ I can see your point about _____. However, I think my success with _____ demonstrates . . .

- → my aptitude.
- → my skill.
- → my motivation.
- → my capability.
- → my resourcefulness.
- → my initiative.
- → my leadership.
- → my risk taking.
- → my organizational skills.

→ Do you think there are real opportunities for me here in the future? What are they?

→ What if . . .

  → next time _____ comes up, we meet and discuss it to decide if it is good timing?

  → I improve _____ by _____? Will that enable me to _____?

→ Based on your feedback, to make up for the skill/knowledge gap, I suggest I . . .

  → take _____ course.

  → get coaching from _____.

  → read up on_____.

  → join _____.

  → go to _____ conference.

→ Let's agree that you are willing to support my development objective of _____.

→ What else should I do to prepare for that opportunity?

Perfect Phrases for Ending Conversations

➜ Thank you so much for hearing me out.

➜ I appreciate your flexibility.

➜ It is a pleasure working with you because I know I can talk straight with you.

➜ I feel really good about this conversation and am reenergized.

➜ I appreciate your coaching and feedback.

CHAPTER 3

Perfect Phrases for Conflict with Peers

The most successful people in business are those who can rally their peers around their cause. Whether you are working in a matrixed global organization or a small local business, your peers can make or break your success. They include anyone in your network, inside or out of your company, who can help you get work done.

It is good practice to think of your peers as customers (or suppliers). For additional ideas on negotiating conflict with your peers, you may also want to look at Chapter 5 on conflicts with customers and vendors.

Perfect Phrases for a Difference of Opinion

When a colleague expresses a point of view that you disagree with, a typical response is to advocate your point of view even more. This can, in fact, escalate the conflict. Instead, try first inquiring about his or her opinion before advocating yours. We have outlined phrases here for both inquiring and advocating:

Inquiring

→ Tell me a little more about that.

→ That disturbs me for some reason. Can you explain it some more?

→ What makes you think that?

→ What do you mean by _____?

→ What led you to this conclusion?

→ Who recommended this?

Advocating

→ I see it differently.

→ Have you considered _____?

→ There are other ways to look at this.

→ May I make another suggestion?

→ Let me further explain why I think this.

→ I insist that . . .

Perfect Phrases for an Unresolved Difference of Opinion

If the combination of inquiring and advocating does not lead to a satisfying resolution of the difference of opinion, and the issue is important to you, you may need to ask for a separate meeting to discuss the matter further.

→ Thank you for taking the time to discuss _____ with me in further detail.

→ I appreciate having the opportunity to further explore _____ with you.

→ It seems that we have two strong, but opposing points of view on _____.

→ I know this topic is important to both of us. I am glad we can take the time to resolve our differences.

→ The way I see it, the objective of this meeting is to see if we can come to a mutually agreeable decision. Do you agree?

→ We know why we are meeting, and _____ is the main topic. Is there anything else we need to discuss related to this?

→ We seem to have different or conflicting objectives based on our roles in the organization. I think we need to discuss what are the criteria for a decision we can both agree to before debating more ideas. This will enable us to spend our energy on coming up with a solution, rather than arguing about positions.

→ This topic has a big impact on . . .

  → collaboration.

  → customer relations.

  → sales volume.

  → profitability.

  → teamwork with _____.

  → our ability to succeed in the market.

  → our reputation with _____.

→ I am sticking with this issue because _____.

→ I feel very passionate about this because _____.

→ We will have a problem if we don't do this because _____.

→ I would like to come to an agreement because _____.

→ Let's set the parameters of the problem. We need to make a decision about _____. The situation is _____. Therefore, any decision we make should address _____, _____, and _____.

→ The criteria for a good decision seem to me to be _____.

→ We are clearly stuck in our position. Let's make sure this is a fight worth fighting. If it is an important issue for both of us, let's take the time to explore why each of us wants what we want. It is the only way to create a win/win solution. This investigation will take time, but it is well worth it.

→ When we spoke last, it was clear that you thought _____, while my opinion was _____. Have you changed your opinion in the meantime?

→ Please explain to me again why you concluded that _____.

→ My opinion is _____. The reason I think this is _____.

→ Let me summarize what I think we have agreed to. The next steps are _____.

→ It seems like we agree that the criteria for a good decision are _____.

→ We also agree on including elements such as _____.

→ Let's come back to this on _____ to discuss further. In the meantime, maybe we can each . . .

  → put together an Excel spreadsheet with our data to discuss next time.

  → make a personal list of pros and cons of each option.

  → brainstorm other alternatives and their implications.

  → create a list of the most important priorities.

  → get input from someone else for some fresh ideas before we reconvene.

  → research best practices in this area.

  → get input from our supervisors.

Perfect Phrases for When Others' Work Habits Disrupt You

Many office places have open, shared work spaces, with cubicles and few offices. The lack of privacy can lead to conflict. The hardest part for people seems to be to bring up the matter in a light-hearted but productive manner.

→ I'm not sure if you are aware of this, but . . .

  → your voice is loud. When I'm on the phone or when I work, I'm distracted by your conversations.

  → your lunches usually smell very strongly. It is quite hard to concentrate during your lunch break.

  → the sound from the videos and music you play is quite loud and distracting.

→ Is there a way you could tone down your voice a little?

→ Would you consider eating in the break room?

→ How about we go to lunch at the same time?

→ Could you get some headphones?

Perfect Phrases for an Abrupt or Impolite Person

It is often the little things that build up and create friction and distance between people at work. Again, the problem is how to bring the issue up and talk about it without the other party feeling like he or she is attacked.

→ This may not be something a lot of people have told you, but since I really appreciate the good relationship we have, I thought I would bring this up. Sometimes you can come across as being impatient or impolite.

→ Were you aware that you can be very abrupt at times?

→ Sometimes, I think you may not be aware that you are abrupt with people.

→ Let me share some specifics with you.

　→ For example, last week at the project meeting you cut off the customer/you jumped in with your point before _____ was finished talking about _____.

　→ Did you realize that you didn't hold the door for the customer when we entered the _____ the other day?

　→ Almost every day, you walk in the office in the morning without saying hello to anybody.

　→ After you cut _____ off, you only got part of the information and may have missed an important part of the context. You may remember, in fact, that later we had to circle back to the same point in the conversation.

→ This can put off people who you may want on your side. In a competitive market, we have to do everything we can to demonstrate that each customer is important to us. Small instances of impoliteness add up and can make our customers think we don't care about them or their business.

→ People respect you, and they may think that you are stressed or in a bad mood when you walk in the office. But they may also think that you are not interested in building good work relationships, promoting collaboration, or engaging in good teamwork.

→ A friendly hello is like a boost of positive energy!

Perfect Phrases for Adverse Comments and Ridicule

When derogatory comments or ridicule are bandied about, it is important to clear the air. It is possible that with differences in humor and personality, you may be taking things personally that are meant in fun. By sharing your perceptions, you can get clear on what is really happening. On the other hand, the approach of subtle jabs, if that is what is happening, needs to be addressed head-on with the person.

→ Look, Joe, we have been working together for X months. You are a key member of the _____ team, and I want you to be satisfied with me and my work. I want to check if you are OK with what I am doing and the contribution I am making to the team.

→ I like to have fun and joke around. I think you do, too.

→ You poke fun at me but I just want to check in if there is something behind the jokes.

→ Do you have some advice for me you are trying to give me behind the jokes? You have been here a long time so I am interested in hearing what you have to say.

→ Has anyone ever told you that you can be . . .

   → very condescending?

   → insulting?

   → demeaning?

→ For instance, when you said _____, you . . .

  → belittled my contribution.

  → made it sound like I was new in the job.

  → highlighted my country/culture/background of origin, implying I was clueless.

→ I have tried to get across to you that your comments are insulting and interfering with my ability to create results. If this happens again, I am going to have to talk with _____.

Perfect Phrases for Peers Who Take Advantage

Beware of parasites. Every organization has them. Address the behavior directly and cut the offenders off unless they reciprocate.

→ I appreciate you reaching out to me for help. Before we go further, I need to share a discomfort I have.

→ You know I am a team player and always happy to help. Sometimes it seems, though, that you are taking advantage.

→ Hi. What can I help you with today? You may be surprised I am greeting you this way. However, it seems that you are always asking for something.

→ Over the last month, you have approached me for . . .

    → a reference for your customer.

    → my old data analysis.

    → assistance with your software.

    → input for a presentation.

    → advice on handling _____.

    → a budget for your project.

→ Yet . . .

    → when I sent you an e-mail and made a follow-up phone call asking for your input on _____, I never heard back from you.

- → when I asked for time to meet about _____, you said you had no time.

- → in our meeting, you quickly shot down my idea for _____.

→ Our give-and-take doesn't feel balanced. What do you think?

→ You are right, you did help me with _____. I apologize for making a big deal of this.

Perfect Phrases for When You're Falsely Blamed

Get your facts together, raise the issue, and ask the other person for a correction. If he or she doesn't comply, pick the key people who should know the truth and inform them. Don't create more noise than necessary. Then move on.

→ I very much appreciate our relationship and admire the way you tackle problems.

→ I have learned a lot from you and appreciate the feedback you give me on a regular basis.

→ You are a great guy! But I'm upset and I need to talk to you.

→ I know you won't like this, but we need to talk about it anyway.

→ This is a very difficult conversation for me to begin, but I need to talk to you.

→ I saw an e-mail that disturbed me.

→ I received an e-mail that didn't make sense to me.

→ I got a message that seems inaccurate.

→ When I walked into the meeting room, I saw this note on the table.

→ It has come to my attention that _____.

→ I have started to hear _____ mentioned to me.

→ I read on _____ that _____.

→ In the e-mail stream, I discovered that you mentioned I didn't _____.

→ In the e-mail I was copied on, I noticed that you said I did _____.

→ During our last conference call, when talking about _____, you were alluding to the fact that I should have _____ when _____. It seems like you didn't agree with the way I handled the situation and you blamed me for _____.

→ From the conversation I had with _____ the other day, I concluded that _____.

→ I'm getting very upset when I hear this. It prevents me from concentrating and being productive.

→ It sends wrong messages around the organization.

→ It feels like I'm losing credibility with people who are key to our mutual success.

→ I may consider quitting. Is this what you want?

→ It makes it very difficult to get the respect from my direct reports and other suppliers, stakeholders, etc.

→ It sounds like you think _____.

→ Did I hear you right when you said _____?

→ Let me clarify. You think that _____?

→ I have a different opinion, but let's look to the future!

→ As I mentioned earlier _____, the fact is that _____.

→ We could discuss this much longer and we may both be right to a certain extent. There are two ways to look at it. However, let's now agree on how we'll work together in the future.

→ I appreciate your candor. It was very important for me to be able to discuss this with you. What should we do in the future to prevent a similar conflict?

→ Thank you for your understanding. I'm glad you could see my point of view.

→ Would you send out an e-mail correcting those rumors?

→ Let's go out with a press release correcting the facts.

→ Let's make sure it doesn't happen again in the future. We'll intervene earlier if we notice anything like that.

→ Please call me directly if you have a question.

→ Please don't speculate! I'm always reachable for you and would be happy to hear from you regularly.

→ I'd be willing to shadow you and see how you are handling similar situations.

→ Shall we create a checklist of how to handle this and similar situations?

→ Let's have regular meetings between you and me. This will allow us to discuss any topic on a regular basis.

→ Please accept that there are times when I can't do it exactly the way you would. There are many ways to solve problems and make a customer happy. We have to be flexible enough to allow multiple methods of doing things and support a creative process, even if it means taking more risk and letting others drive the process.

→ Let's meet with _____ and get his opinion as well.

Perfect Phrases for When You're Not Included in Critical Situations

Use these phrases to find out why you were not included and to request to be included next time.

→ Hi, Christopher. Thanks for agreeing to talk today. This is really important for the _____ project.

→ I thought it was best if we discussed this in person.

→ I am having some problems with the _____ project.

→ You may not know that . . .

   → I have been heavily involved in the _____ project.

   → my role in the _____ project is _____.

   → I just got assigned to _____.

   → I am the assigned subject matter expert for _____.

   → I was the originator of _____.

   → I am responsible for _____.

   → my bonus is attached to _____.

   → I have been the interface to this customer.

→ I know that you . . .

   → have been heavily involved in the _____ project.

   → just got assigned to _____.

- → are the assigned subject matter expert for _____.
- → were the originator of _____.
- → are responsible for _____.
→ I heard through _____ that _____.
→ I read the minutes of the last meeting with _____.
→ When talking to _____, he referred to a meeting I was not aware of.
→ I saw the slide deck for _____ meeting and I was surprised about how many new ideas were incorporated that I never had input on.
→ You shared the specifics about _____ with me ____ weeks after the fact.
→ I read in the newsletter about the new _____.
→ I was approached by _____ for a budget for _____.
→ I looked stupid in the _____ meeting when I did not know about _____.
→ It makes our team look bad when I ask a question that I should have known the answer to.
→ I was unable to complete _____ properly.
→ Our customer is getting confused by the mixed messages.
→ I reported incorrect information in my last monthly report to _____.
→ So you are saying _____?

→ Did you mean _____?

→ Wait a minute. You think that _____?

→ Thank you for hearing me out. I was very upset, but I now feel better.

→ We live in a fast-paced environment. Things can get overlooked. I understand you didn't do it intentionally.

→ Now I better understand the challenges you are facing in this role.

→ Don't worry about it. No big harm done. Let's discuss how to avoid this in future.

→ I hope you understand this has major negative consequences on _____. We'll probably be able to recover, but this was a big mistake.

→ I am very disappointed. I'll need a little time to process this before we talk some more.

→ In the future, you will include me on _____ before taking action.

→ For the next project, let's meet when we start and clearly define roles, responsibilities, and the decision-making process.

→ In the future, please send me a draft of _____ before going out with communication.

→ I'd like to be cc'd on anything that relates to _____.

→ This is something that can happen once, but it is serious.

→ I am going to need to talk to _____ to see how to work this out.

Perfect Phrases for an Unresponsive Colleague

In the fast-paced world we work in, it is common for colleagues to have to confront the issue of unresponsiveness. For example, you may have left voice mails and sent e-mails but are not getting any reply. What do you do?

If it is a peer in the same office who is not getting back to you, try to find him or her and talk face-to-face. However, if your colleague works in another location, you will want to call and send an e-mail request to have a conversation. If you are not successful with those repeated attempts, approach him or her as below.

It is helpful in these situations to share the impression the lack of responsiveness is making. Sharing this personal point of view often opens up the dialogue.

→ I really appreciate you taking the time for this.

→ It seems like we had some issues. My hope is we can straighten this out today.

→ I really need your input and collaboration on this.

→ I came here today so we can find a solution going forward to meet both our needs.

→ You have not been responding to my e-mails or voice mails. My guess is that . . .

    → you are on vacation.

    → it's not important to you.

- → you don't have the answer I have been requesting from you.
- → you may have technology problems.
- → I'd very much appreciate hearing from you and collaboratively finding a way to best address both our needs.
- → This is very important to me/to our business/to the success of our project/for the proposal phase we are in because . . .
  - → the next action item is on the critical path and I can't proceed without having spoken to you.
  - → by not speaking we are potentially losing _____ per day.
  - → I can't be responsive to my customers and they again may interpret it as a lack of interest or courtesy.
- → I have had a difficult time lately. I have been stressed out/ overloaded/putting out fires/frustrated because . . .
  - → when I asked you for additional resources, you didn't get back to me.
  - → my communication about availability for our meeting went unanswered.
  - → my voice mail asking for permission to spend $X on _____ was not responded to.
- → This is a critical situation because . . .
  - → I couldn't reply to my customer's request.
  - → I may have made wrong pricing decisions.

→ I may not have billed the right amount.

→ I missed the deadline.

→ I looked bad in front of _____ because it looked like I didn't have my act together.

→ I recognize you have other priorities.

→ I know you have a lot going on.

→ I am sure there are reasons I haven't heard from you.

→ My personal goal is to get back to people in some shape or form within twenty-four hours. That doesn't mean I have all the answers but at least I want to give them something. Do you support me in this goal?

→ My understanding is that we are equal partners on this project. This means that we need to each do our share to keep the other updated. What can I do to keep you better informed? What I need from you is _____.

→ I know we have been exchanging a lot of e-mails. But we are working on the same floor. I suggest that once per _____ we meet for lunch to stay updated.

→ I know we are in different time zones and so far away. This makes e-mail easier. However I would like to speak by phone once per _____. What timing works for you?

→ What alternatives can you suggest to improve responsiveness?

→ How do you collaborate with others to keep them updated?

Perfect Phrases for an Uncollaborative Peer

Rare but tough situations. Either sit it out or address it directly. If you address it, have enough examples ready to make your case. The following are some phrases to help.

➔ I want to bring something up with you. Don't take this the wrong way. It seems like we are at odds with _____ project. I would rather it not be that way.

➔ Let me share some examples.

  ➔ During the _____ meeting, you presented ideas as yours that we developed together.

  ➔ When you presented the project to _____, you were saying I instead of we.

  ➔ Only after the fact and accidently did I hear about the meeting you had with _____ to discuss _____.

  ➔ You didn't include me in _____.

  ➔ You are very slow to respond to requests for information, such as _____.

  ➔ During lunch with _____ you couldn't stop making jokes at my expense.

  ➔ When we met with customer X, you didn't bother to introduce me.

  ➔ When we worked late the other day, you only ordered dinner for yourself and the team but not for me.

- ➜ You send me e-mails about problems and copy the team instead of coming to my office to discuss them.

- ➜ You sent an e-mail to the executive committee with all our achievements without copying me or the team.

➜ At last week's staff meeting, you made the case that your tasks were more important than mine, when it seems to me that they both are integral to the project's success. Tell me where you are coming from.

➜ I think as a team we can gain more by collaborating as colleagues than by competing.

➜ Let's talk about some ways we can collaborate on _____.

➜ A little competition is healthy, and I don't mind it. However, are you willing to agree on how to collaborate?

➜ Our jobs do intersect. Some important areas for me to be able to work with you are . . .

- ➜ getting updated on _____.

- ➜ sharing information that the others can use on their project.

- ➜ responding positively to requests for help.

➜ What can I do to be more collaborative?

➜ If we can't work this out, I am going to need to speak with our manager because I cannot work this way anymore.

Perfect Phrases for a Peer Who Challenges Your Expertise

Listen to your colleague and see what you can learn about why he or she is challenging your expertise. If you need to defend yourself, choose a mix of hard and soft credentials to back up your ideas. Don't delay, as this peer may be working to undermine your ideas.

→ Thank you for your comment. I hadn't seen it that way. That helps me to better understand what is going on.

→ Thank you. Let me chew on it. I'll get back to you tomorrow.

→ Thank you for the feedback. Tell me more what you mean.

→ Those are really good points. May I include them in my analysis?

→ I appreciate your insight. Can we leverage your knowledge for the next project?

→ Wait a minute, that is not true.

→ I believe you have your facts mixed up.

→ Your point is very well taken. I am happy you are mentioning that. It allows me to restate our rationale that led to this idea.

→ Thank you for raising the issue. I know this is a complex topic. Let's review the data we have and the conclusions we can make.

→ The fact is . . .

  → this approach has worked on _____.

  → our competitor is doing _____ and it has resulted in _____.

  → if you look at the industry/association database, you will see that _____.

  → in your own presentation last week you highlighted _____, which is based on the same thinking.

  → when I spoke with _____ in _____, he referred to their best practice. This is very similar to what I am suggesting.

  → in our last customer survey, customers expressed _____.

  → if you take the pain to review _____, you will find a lot of answers to the questions you have raised.

  → at my former employer _____, we did exactly this very successfully.

  → there is a growing body of research that points to _____. Why would we wait until someone steals the idea first?

  → our engineering department made an extensive feasibility study that showed encouraging results. You can find them at _____.

  → a pilot is under way. We will have final results by _____. As of last week, the results have been _____.

→ we have hired the best _____ to support the success of this.

→ this is not based on my idea, it is building on input we received from _____, a leading industry expert.

→ Some of you don't know me; let me give a summary of my experience. I do this not to put myself on center stage but just to give you an understanding of what is behind these ideas.

  → I have worked at _____.

  → My key achievements at a previous company included _____.

  → My original research in the area includes _____.

  → The relevant customers I have worked with are _____.

  → See my blog on the topic at _____.

  → I have written some articles/books on the topic, including _____.

→ I suggest you look at those materials and we meet again on _____ to discuss this more. How long do you need?

→ I would be happy to answer any questions you have. Please send them to me by _____.

→ I will answer any questions by _____ and we can reconvene on _____ to make a decision.

Perfect Phrases for Challenging Your Peer's Expertise

Challenging a peer's expertise is a delicate situation in which you risk being wrong. In the interest of ensuring the integrity of his or her ideas, use these phrases to test your peer's qualifications.

→ How did you come to that conclusion?

→ Can you please explain further?

→ Can you help me by giving me more background on . . .

  → the data?

  → your analysis?

  → the people you spoke with?

→ This is a very interesting perspective. Can you explain the process you went through to come to this conclusion?

→ I wouldn't have thought of that. Tell me . . .

  → how this has worked in similar situations?

  → of a project where you have done something similar?

  → if you have done this before?

→ Have you discussed your findings with _____?

→ Interesting. This seems to be contrary to what I . . .

  → heard from _____.

  → learned from _____.

  → experienced when _____.

→ What other options have you considered?

→ How does what you are saying compare with the . . .

  → findings of _____?

  → latest research from _____?

  → best practices of _____?

  → industry standards?

→ It sounds like your assumptions are _____. I am looking to create a solution that addresses _____. Let's talk about this for a minute.

→ I have been doing this for years and know our customer base. I speak to them every day. I have doubts that they would agree with this.

→ Thank you for this refreshing look at _____. I need to process it a little more. Can you send me the slides?

→ That won't work here. You are based out of _____. We have a completely different market here.

→ I appreciate your comments. However, I don't think you are qualified to draw that conclusion.

→ Once we get this additional information, I would be delighted to review it and reconvene.

Perfect Phrases for Dealing with a Colleague You Don't Trust

Trust is a key ingredient of any collaboration. You must resolve it before proceeding. Use these phrases to address your concerns.

→ We have not worked together before and I am a little worried. This is a high-visibility project and I want it to succeed.

→ Let's talk about our . . .

  → goals.

  → standards.

  → communication plan.

  → criteria for our deliverables: quality, quantity, and time.

→ How have you worked on similar projects? What have you learned that we can apply here?

→ I am very detailed and even a certain level of perfectionist. How would you characterize yourself?

→ This is going to be very difficult for me. There are so many other things happening in parallel. I am commit-ted to do everything it takes to make this a success. However, these are some things I am going to need from you: _____. What could I do to help you?

→ I know we are both very busy with many priorities. We will have to align ourselves very closely. I suggest we make a detailed project plan with deliverables, time lines, and quality measures. This will help us stay on target. Also, I suggest we set up a regular meeting schedule to help keep us on track.

→ We worked together on _____. It didn't go as well as I had hoped. What can we do to prevent this?

→ Before we start this new project, I would appreciate it if we could take a few minutes and debrief the last one. While in the end we did get it done, I had a slight problem with _____. Do you remember how that happened? Can you tell me where you were coming from?

→ Let's get started as soon as possible and check in on _____. Based on the results of this first step, we can evaluate the effectiveness of our collaboration and decide how to proceed.

→ I have asked _____ to support you by doing _____. Don't hesitate to contact either of us with questions along the way.

→ I know this is a tricky issue to address. Since this is such an important project, let me just address it very openly. I have doubts whether you are up to this, because . . .

  → you don't have _____ skills.

  → your network is limited.

  → you have never done this before.

  → you don't have the seniority.

  → _____ doesn't like you.

→ You really need to convince me that this will work before we go forward.

→ Please don't take this personally. But since I do not know you well enough and I don't want to take a risk on such an important project, I am not willing to partner with you unless you _____. Please let me know how you are going to do this.

CHAPTER 4

Perfect Phrases for Conflict with Employees

Conflict with employees usually boils down to problems with their behavior. They are late, they are not pulling their weight, they are contradicting you, and so on.

For the most effective approach to resolving these conflicts, first fine-tune the "Raise the Issue" section of your dialogue to include sharing:

■ **What you want the employee to do.** This is helpful to frame the conversation on the business goal at hand. It sets a positive tone and also is a chance to reiterate your expectations and vision for him or her, providing the big picture for the conversation to remind your employee this is not a personal attack but is about work and results.

■ **What you have seen the employee doing.** After you have set the goal, you can share specifically what you have seen him or her doing and how it is not meeting your expectation.

■ **What the impact is of his or her current behavior.** This final step is critical. It tells the employee the impact of their behavior on you, the team, the customer, the project, the company, and so on. This reminds your employee that he or she operates within a system and his or her behavior impacts others. This will help motivate him or her to change the behavior in question.

Sometimes the conflict can be ongoing. Perhaps you already spoke to him or her about a problem or issue and it still is not resolved. If this is the case, we suggest you add the following:

1. **Opening.** Restate the conclusions of your previous conversations with this person.

2. **Share specifics.** Give the latest example of how he or she is not meeting the previous agreement as well as the impact it is having.

3. **Closing.** Resecure his or her commitment to changing. Remind your employee why it is important he or she change the behavior in question. You may even need to let him or her know the consequences of not changing. Create an action plan and schedule a follow-up meeting.

Perfect Phrases for Opening a Conflict Discussion with an Employee

When an employee gets brought in to speak to a manager, it is natural for him or her to feel anxious. Starting by setting a positive tone and then focus on the reason for the discussion.

→ I really appreciate your input to our team.

→ I have great respect for your talents and skills.

→ You're adding a lot of value.

→ I am so happy you have come up to speed quickly.

→ I have asked to speak with you . . .

  → with the goal of becoming an even more valuable resource.

  → with the purpose of helping you to add even more to your team.

  → in the spirit of immediate feedback.

  → to discuss some of my observations.

Perfect Phrases for an Underperforming Employee

There are many reasons why an employee may not perform up to expectations. No matter the reason, address it as soon as possible to uncover problems so you can mitigate them.

→ We may have had a misunderstanding as I may not have been clear about my expectations.

→ I do not expect anyone on this team to be perfect. We all make mistakes.

→ What I am looking for is . . .

- → quick tabulation of new ideas after our meetings.

- → a high-level design document complying with our design methodology.

- → that you address issues with customers right away.

- → that you come up with concrete plans based on my high-level ideas to be done by _____.

- → that you dress appropriately for the _____.

- → that you arrive before everyone else to get things set up.

- → that you keep me up to date on _____ without me having to ask.

- → that you alert me as soon as there is a possibility that something could go wrong with _____ and not wait until after the fact.

- → that you be positive and supportive of _____.

→ What happened is . . .

> → I met with you _____ and we had an extended discussion about how we could address _____. You seemed to be clear that you were going to tabulate the new ideas and get back to everyone on the team. I haven't heard from you since. The impact is we are losing momentum and may not be able to hit the next deadline.

> → the document I received from you doesn't comply with our design methodology, specifically _____. If you are not complying with this methodology, then others will not follow either. This will seriously hamper what we have set out to do in setting standards.

> → I was disturbed to receive a call from customer _____. Our agreement is _____ and usually you are very responsive. However, it doesn't appear you took any action. This is shedding a very bad light on our overall services and jeopardizing our image as a "premium" supplier.

> → we discussed my idea of creating a new _____ during our last strategy meeting. You seemed all for it and very excited. You also agreed to scope out specific features and design criteria as you usually do. We had set the deadline by the end of last week. Are you still working on it? Any more delay will make it harder to pitch it with our executive committee since there is a meeting on _____ where I had intended to present our ideas.

→ consulting the _____ needed to be done by you by _____. It has not. My boss and the customer are up in arms!

→ at the _____ conference we had the _____ meeting with this group of prospects. As we casually were sitting at those cocktail tables, I noticed that your shoes looked very dirty and also that the color did not match your suit. It may seem like a small detail to you, but the way we dress sends signals of our overall attitude and how we approach things. I suggest you pay more attention to your shoes in the future.

→ I was very nervous ahead of our board meeting presentation last week. We had talked about its importance and I was relying on you to help me with the technology. When you didn't show up until fifteen minutes before the meeting started, I was very nervous and upset. It may have jeopardized the success of our presentation.

→ I was very hesitant to ask you about the latest _____ report this morning. We had agreed you would inform me automatically. It just unnecessarily adds to my workload to have to go looking for the information.

→ I was very surprised when I ran into _____ yesterday and he started talking about the _____ production problem. That I was not aware of it made

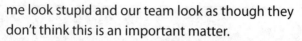

me look stupid and our team look as though they don't think this is an important matter.

→ your reaction in today's meeting showed a lot of the negative elements we had discussed earlier. You started questioning our criteria for decision making, suddenly brought up completely new arguments, and didn't want to commit. This is dragging down your fellow teammates, and it unnecessarily extended the meeting.

→ How do you see it?

→ How did you experience this situation?

→ What's your point of view?

→ How do you feel about this?

→ What are your thoughts?

→ What ideas do you have to prevent this in the future?

→ How can we collaborate for success next time?

→ What could you do to make sure this doesn't happen again?

→ What is your plan?

→ What can I do to help?

→ What could I do differently next time?

Perfect Phrases for a Negative Employee

Negativity is toxic. Addressing it head-on and specifically goes a long way to not only resolve your conflict but also to create a more productive work environment for everyone.

→ Let me preface this conversation by saying that I am not looking for employees who say yes to everything I say/our customers say/each other suggests. However, it is much more productive and enjoyable to have people who see the glass half full, not half empty.

→ We all need to support the ideas we agree to as a team.

→ We should try to be more open to suggestions anybody makes about improvement. It will get us a long way.

→ Listening nondefensively to feedback from our customers is very important.

→ We have to avoid always finding what is wrong and never looking at what is working.

→ Talking negatively behind other people's backs is a no-no.

→ We can't work with leaders who are supportive in public but not in private.

→ It seems unacceptable to me that during a meeting you are positive, but afterward you go around and talk negatively about what we decided.

→ A smile makes a huge difference! Try to see life and our business from the bright side.

→ Let's try to make a balanced statement instead of mentioning as our first reaction what is negative.

→ Last meeting we agreed to _____ to address _____. You seemed to be comfortable with the decision and did not voice any concerns. Now I am hearing reports that you have been bad-mouthing this decision. The impact is that our organization will not support our decision, and our colleagues on our team will be reluctant to support anything we decide in the future.

→ Last Friday, your peer _____ brought a draft Power Point presentation to show to the team. You spent ten minutes focusing on all of the small errors such as typos and slide formatting when we had only thirty minutes for the meeting. This prevented us from having a constructive conversation about the concepts in the presentation and also left your peer humiliated.

→ Whenever _____ brings up a new idea, you roll your eyes! I fear he or she will soon not make any more suggestions.

→ Every morning when you walked by my desk last week, you had a frown on your face and didn't say hello to anybody. It drags me down, since it makes me wonder what is potentially wrong with you but also with the team or me.

→ I was shocked when we had that conversation at lunch yesterday and you did nothing but highlight the negative characteristics of people. Collaborating with you will be very difficult when you only see people's weaknesses.

→ I became frustrated in our last strategy meeting when for each idea that was brought up, you only found the reasons why it would not work. At the same time, you did not offer any of your own suggestions. This puts you in a bad light and will not get you very far.

→ Are you aware of the fact that you come across as negative?

→ What has precipitated this negative behavior of yours?

→ How did you experience the situation I'm describing?

→ Do you agree that you have to break this pattern? How are you going to do it? How can I help? Would you want some coaching?

→ What ideas do you have to prevent this in the future?

Perfect Phrases for an Employee Requesting More Money, Resources, or Time

Requests for "more" are often multifaceted. Make sure you know what is behind it before you agree.

→ I appreciate the effort you put into your daily work. I understand that you have requested help on meeting your deadlines. I know sometimes it feels as if there is not enough time in the day.

→ I appreciate the hard work you are putting in on this project. I understand you need more resources for _____.

→ First of all, let me tell you I am impressed by all the projects you are taking on. At the same time, we have to be careful that we don't overstretch our capacities. This is true for people, money, and other resources. It is your job to reallocate your fixed budget in such a way that you can fund your projects according to your priorities. Something has to give.

→ It seems that you have the resources but you need to reallocate them to the right projects. You can put more into _____, but you will need to take it from somewhere else.

→ I received your message that you are stretched too thin and need more resources. Please explain.

→ What data do you have to justify needing more resources?

→ What has changed since the initial planning?

→ I don't want to be insensitive to your request, but you must understand that we are squeezed for money. Help me understand more specifically what is driving your request.

→ I understand there is a lot to do. Our job is to figure out how to prioritize tasks so we can get everything done. How can I help you prioritize?

→ Don't get me wrong. I want you to be successful. I depend on you. What can I do to help you succeed within the constraints we have?

→ Let me hear more about how you are handling _____. Maybe there are some tricks I can share with you.

→ I think there may some efficiencies you could gain by speaking with _____. Let me contact them to let them know that you will be reaching out to them.

→ You might want to check with _____ who may have time/money/resources to help you.

→ I know there are others in our team who are carrying a similar workload with similar resources. How can you explain the difference?

→ We need to be looking for ways to make it happen, not reasons why it can't happen.

→ Thank you for bringing this up. I know there is no magic answer. Please keep giving it your best.

→ These conversations help me understand the challenges you are facing.

→ I hope this has helped you understand the environment we are working in.

→ Please keep your mind open to unconventional solutions.

→ Yours is not an easy task. However, let me be clear that the expectation is that you will finish this project on time and on budget. Keep me posted on how it is going.

Perfect Phrases for a Noncompliant Employee

There is a fine line between misunderstanding and insubordination. Be crystal clear of your expectations with your employee before assuming the latter.

➔ Based on what we agreed, my expectation was . . .

  ➔ that the delivery was to shipped by _____.

  ➔ the invoice was to be submitted by _____.

  ➔ the project was to be completed by _____.

  ➔ you would meet with _____ and discuss _____.

➔ What happened is . . .

  ➔ the delivery is sitting in the warehouse.

  ➔ the invoice is open.

  ➔ the project is behind schedule.

  ➔ I just got a call from _____ complaining that he has not heard from you.

➔ The impact of this is . . .

  ➔ we now have an angry customer who told me that since we have not followed through on our commitment he or she is considering canceling future orders.

  ➔ our cash account is depleted.

  ➔ my manager just chewed me out because he made commitments based on our project plans.

→ we have lost credibility with _____, a key internal opinion leader.

→ our team's reputation is being damaged.

→ the promotion that we discussed for you is in jeopardy because you have shown yourself to be unreliable.

→ What happened?

→ What were the key contributors to this situation?

→ Did you understand my initial instructions?

→ How come you didn't follow through as we had agreed?

→ Why didn't you let me know this was going on?

→ Do you think you have the skills and tools to handle this?

→ Why didn't you seek assistance from _____?

→ What are you planning to do to address this problem?

→ What can you do to make sure this doesn't happen again?

→ What can I do to help you succeed next time?

→ What measures can we take to prevent this from getting so far out of control next time?

→ What, if anything, can I do differently next time?

→ What would you do if you were in my place?

Perfect Phrases for a Confrontational Employee

To confront a confrontational person takes a lot of guts. Trust your instincts and stand up for your beliefs.

→ This may not be an easy conversation, but it is very important we can talk openly and candidly with each other. Are you up for it?

→ How are you? How have the last few weeks been for you?

→ Our company values are based on mutual respect and courtesy.

→ We treat each other with respect.

→ Through all my years at _____, we have been very strict when observing harassment and other violations of our company code.

→ Not only our company but many companies want to create a friendly work environment for employees.

→ (Name) told me that in graduate school you were already known for your outbursts. But since then you have greatly improved and until as recently as last month _____ was commending your great attitude.

→ I have observed multiple occasions when you were very rude and confrontational with your colleagues. For instance, when we were in the _____ meeting the other day, you very abruptly interrupted _____ and reprimanded him or her for not being thoroughly prepared.

→ I received a complaint from _____ that you were lashing out at your office neighbor for talking too loudly on the phone.

→ When walking up the stairs last evening, I overheard the conversation you had with _____ about his or her approach to _____. You sounded condescending. Even if he or she does things differently than you, we welcome diversity and different approaches to problem solving.

→ I don't know if you are aware of it, but even now, when talking to me, your voice takes on a threatening tone. It is intimidating to many in our office.

→ Also, if you don't mind, let's look at some of your e-mails I have in my in-box. Here is one you have sent to _____. What do you think about it? If you were in his or her shoes and I wrote to you like that, would you appreciate it?

→ The consequence is that we are running the risk of damaging our great team spirit.

→ It is creating an environment of fear.

→ You know that I have been a big supporter of you throughout the years you have been with us. However, it's becoming more and more difficult.

→ People are asking me to not put them on your project team.

→ We lost _____, a very valuable employee. In the exit interview, he mentioned the rough work environment in your team.

Perfect Phrases for an Employee Setting the Wrong Priorities

It is critical to clear up prioritization misalignments right away. In today's world of more work than time, even a short period of misaligned priorities can set back a whole team or project. It is a major cause of failed projects.

➔ I am aware of the fact that we are asking more and more from everyone.

➔ I know that you have a few new projects on your plate. Your plate probably feels full.

➔ Let's take a few minutes and walk through your priorities so we can make sure you are not overwhelmed.

➔ Tell me what you understand to be your top priorities.

➔ What is on your list that you can say "no" to?

➔ What do you think you can get done by the end of the day/week/month?

➔ Please tell me what you have completed in the last day/week/month?

➔ What have you understood from me to be your top priority?

➔ I am very pleased with all the work you have completed recently. At the same time, I notice you are working very long hours. I want to make sure you are not killing yourself. Let's walk through your priorities.

→ I don't want to be perceived as a micromanager. But I thought it might be a good idea if you walked me through your current workload and priorities so that you are focused on the most important items.

→ Our goal is a balanced workload across the team.

→ Our team approach is to make sure that we have a reasonable balance of work and life.

→ You need to have a breather to be able to think creatively and add value to this project.

→ I want to make sure you are able to keep up your work pace over the long term.

→ You are right, _____ is a critical project.

→ I know you don't want to hear this right now; however, I need your skills on _____.

→ Who can we get to help you with _____ so that we can get you on _____?

→ I see it this way. Your number-one priority is _____ because _____.

→ I disagree with the way you set your priorities. We both know what has happened in the past. I want to prevent _____ for both your and the team's benefit.

→ You cannot take on _____ now. Project _____ is highly critical right now because _____. Let's look at getting you some time on that next week.

→ When you decided to take on _____, what was your objective/vision?

→ What was your plan for _____ as you worked
   on _____?

→ Have you thought where you will be with your team three
   months from now? How would you be perceived if you
   can continue focusing on _____?

→ Please send me an e-mail with your updated project plan.

→ Let's touch base next week to review your success with
   this new plan.

→ In the meantime, if any priority conflicts arise, please contact me so we can collaborate on a solution.

Perfect Phrases for an Employee Who Doesn't Follow Up

Addressing compliance issues and delays are critical to creating high performance. Handling them quickly sends a clear message to the employee and the whole team.

→ We talked about this last _____. You said you would contact me by _____ with an update. You didn't. What happened?

→ What prevented you from telling me sooner?

→ It sometimes feels like you intentionally leave me out of the loop because you don't want me looking over your shoulder.

→ Since I need to update my manager on our team's projects, I need to know what progress you are making on a daily/weekly/monthly basis.

→ We lost face/money/credibility because I did not hear from you in time.

→ I find it hard to trust you right now based on your repetitive breaches of our agreement.

→ That is not what I meant. Let me clarify.

→ I misunderstood you. I thought you said _____.

→ What can we do the next time so that I get what I need?

→ Is what I am asking you to do reasonable?

→ How would you react if you were in my shoes?

→ Why is it so difficult to follow up? Please explain.

→ Maybe you can talk to _____ for some ideas. She does an excellent job of keeping me posted.

→ This is not acceptable. If I ask for an update, I need to get it. As a result, I will have to _____.

→ Going forward, I will need to hear from you every _____. I know this may feel like micromanaging. However, until you can consistently follow through on your commitments, I need to monitor you more closely.

Perfect Phrases for an Employee Who Doesn't Follow Through

Accountability is a key indicator of teamwork. Employees must be held to their word.

→ I need to address this with you, and it may not be an easy conversation. It seems like you are having a hard time following through on _____.

→ What is triggering this conversation is project _____, in which you had committed to deliver _____ by _____.

→ I received a phone call/e-mail from _____ that you have not been following through on _____.

→ By not following through, you are jeopardizing . . .

  → the success of this project.

  → the reputation of your team.

  → profitability.

  → your reputation.

  → your ability to gain others' trust.

→ What held you back from meeting your commitment?

→ What, if anything, could I have done to have helped you overcome that barrier?

→ How can you make sure this doesn't happen in the future?

→ What can I do to support you?

→ Please tell me about your most successful project where you met all of your commitments.

→ Do you mind if I check in with you regularly? It would go a long way toward increasing my confidence level.

→ Please send me a daily/weekly progress report so I can review your status.

→ I will check once a week to make sure your project manager is getting what he or she needs from you.

→ I want you to meet weekly with _____ as a mentor to help you stay organized.

→ You either need to be able to manage your workload so that you can follow through on commitments or we have to _____.

Perfect Phrases for a Chronically Late Employee

Timeliness has a lot to do with courtesy and productivity. You have to set the standard by being on time yourself and challenging those who are late.

→ Is there something new that has come up that is making you consistently late?

→ Here, at _____ company, we value being on time. What was it like at your last job?

→ I am completely at a loss. What is it going to take to get you here on time?

→ Being late not only violates our policy. Your colleagues suffer from an increased workload covering for you.

→ You are late again. I am not sure whether you know, but to me this says "I am not important." I take your being late very personally.

→ Do you know what time our meeting was supposed to start?

→ It is not only that you arrive late. Usually, your contributions suffer from the missed conversations.

→ It takes time to mentally prepare and transition into a meeting. I need you to do that before the meeting, not during the meeting.

→ Your delay slows us all down. We have to spend time getting you up to speed.

→ Do not come up with excuses of traffic or a surprise visitor. You have to build such surprises into your plan to be able to arrive on time.

→ Do you realize how much money we just wasted? There are _____ people in this meeting waiting for you.

→ Our goal is start on time and end on time.

→ You might want to try arriving fifteen minutes early. You may find yourself less stressed and more productive.

→ We are going to try a new approach. Once the meeting starts, the door closes and no one will be allowed to enter.

Perfect Phrases for an Uncommitted Employee

Creating a trusting environment allows for differences of opinion to emerge. Look first to make sure you are creating an environment where employees can disagree with you.

→ You are saying one thing and doing another.

→ You are sending conflicting messages to the team/ customer.

→ I need to meet with you about something that is reducing our team productivity.

→ I am happy to discuss any objection you have to ideas and go through all considerations while we are meeting. Once we leave with a decision, though, I expect you to support it.

→ What is preventing you from bringing up your objections during the meetings?

→ You have said "I didn't say/do that" before. The fact is that your statements and behaviors are interpreted differently.

→ It is not just me that is getting this impression. Others have come to me with similar concerns.

→ What do you think you agreed to at the last meeting?

→ What did you say that could have been misconstrued as not supporting the management decision?

→ I would like to meet with you before each meeting for the next week/month/quarter to discuss your thoughts and concerns so we can address them during the meeting.

→ We are going to begin writing down decisions on the whiteboard and getting a thumbs up/thumbs down from everyone before we leave.

→ At our next conference call, I am going to ask everyone directly if they support the decision before we end the call. This will give you the space to discuss your objections.

Perfect Phrases for a Contradictory Employee

Contradictions are key ingredients of an open discussion. However, raised at the wrong time, with the wrong intensity, or with the wrong person, they will backfire.

→ I am referring back to our meeting with _____ on _____.

→ I very much appreciate your point of view. You may not have noticed, but you have repeatedly contradicted me. For instance, _____.

→ I welcome different points of view and animated discussions. As far as your contradictions, however, I take them personally.

→ It seems like you are treating me differently: you are particularly critical of my comments. For instance, _____.

→ Am I wrong, or is it that when I bring up a suggestion, you bring up the opposite idea? For example, _____.

→ I don't bring this up lightly, and I don't want to come across as overly sensitive. However, I interpret this as resisting my leadership.

→ What you are saying is possible, but I don't want to give you an easy way out just yet. I need to know there is nothing else behind it.

→ What do you think about what I am saying?

→ The tensions between you and me come at the expense of team productivity. For instance, our discussion about _____ took much longer than it could have. I am not saying I am perfect, but you and I have to find the solution together. What do you suggest?

→ Is there something about the timing or the tone of my comments that disturbed you?

→ Presenting a consistent message to _____ is very important. _____ is a key customer.

→ We look like we are not prepared when you contradict me in these meetings.

→ It makes us look like our company does not agree internally when you contradict me in meetings.

→ I feel like I lose credibility when you contradict me in front of other departments.

→ It feels like you are challenging my authority when you contradict me in front of _____.

→ We are not providing a unified voice to the customer when you openly contradict me.

→ For decisions regarding _____, I am the final word. For decisions regarding _____, you can feel free to challenge me.

→ I hear that you thought this was an open discussion. That is not the case at all.

→ I understand that in our team meetings, we debate openly. Customer meetings, however, are completely different.

→ I am open to discussing your point of view before or after meetings with _____. However, it is not acceptable in front of _____.

Perfect Phrases for Dealing with an Employee Complaining About a Colleague

→ Yes, I know who you are talking about and what situation you are referring to.

→ Have you talked to him or her about it?

→ I'm not really comfortable discussing a third person with you. It feels like no matter what I say it may be wrong. I'd be happy to help if you have any specific requests for me, but I think you should discuss it with _____ directly.

→ I have no doubt that this is something you will be able to figure out between the two of you. Do you need any coaching?

CHAPTER 5

Perfect Phrases for Conflict with Customers and Vendors

I s your customer always king? Do you have to do whatever he or she is asking for? Or can you take a stand and push back? There are no perfect answers but here is one guiding principle: it is a partnership.

When conflict arises with customers, it feels like a potential death threat. However, no good customer has an interest in doing anything that would jeopardize the health of you or your business. Make sure your customers (or vendors) understand the implications of their requests. Good customers will be willing to discuss options with you. And if it is a personality issue, get help from a peer you trust or your boss. Oftentimes it's just about being heard! Practice your listening skills. Don't get defensive.

Perfect Phrases for Unreasonable Requests from Customers

A customer calls you and complains about your product or services. He or she expected a delivery date/price/quality specification that seems unreasonable. You fear losing the customer if you don't comply. Use these phrases to handle the situation.

➜ The last thing I want to say is "no."

➜ There must be something we can work out. I hope you know by now that we are positive, flexible, creative, and customer focused.

➜ This is not as simple as it seems. Let me look into that. It will take me _____ to research options, discuss ideas with colleagues, and prepare an effective response.

➜ Based on my experience and knowledge in this area, that might be incredibly difficult to achieve. But before I pass judgment, let me do some research.

➜ Can you tell me more about why you need that quality/time line/price?

➜ Let me investigate and get back to you with what I discover.

➜ Why don't we schedule a follow-up call on _____ to discuss options. How about _____?

➜ I looked into this issue, and it is something that will take more than a phone call to resolve. You are a very important customer to us. Let's meet for lunch and discuss some creative solutions.

→ I looked into your request and here is what I found . . .

→ We have several options:

> → We can deliver by that date, but it will cost _____ extra.

> → We can reduce the quality to _____ and meet your deadline.

> → We can produce _____ amount by that deadline and the rest by _____.

> → If you can set up the trucking, we can produce your order by _____.

→ Which of these options is best for you?

→ It seems like if we can just do _____, we can make this work for you.

→ It sounds like what is most important is _____.

→ I understand that you are willing to pay _____ for this special order, but only this time.

→ I realize none of these options are exactly what you are looking for. In the future, if we can _____, then we will be able to meet similar requests.

→ This has to be done because of your customer's needs, so it may help to talk to my manager.

→ OK, let's agree to do _____.

→ As a next step, I'm going to talk to _____.

→ Can you please verify with Purchasing if _____.

→ Thank you for listening! I'm sure we'll be able to fix this problem. We appreciate your loyalty as a customer.

→ I will talk to our internal customer service and get _____ done.

→ I am happy to have you speak with my manager. If you can wait on hold for two minutes, I will update him or her on the details of the conversation before you reach him or her. Or, if you would like, I can have my manager call you.

Perfect Phrases for a Customer Left Out of the Loop

If you have received a customer complaint by e-mail, think twice before replying by e-mail. In many cases, it is best to pick up the phone.

→ I'm calling in reference to the e-mail I received from you today in which you raised the issue of not having been involved in the discussion between _____ and me.

→ I apologize for any bad feelings I may have caused. It was not my intention to go behind your back.

→ I appreciate our relationship tremendously. It is important to me that you understand what my considerations were when I did not include you in this conversation.

→ Our project charter says _____.

→ The contract defines that _____.

→ My understanding was you did not want to be involved in this part of every operational implementation and just wanted to hear about the milestones.

→ My understanding was that you were on vacation.

→ You must have been really offended by me not telling you what I'm doing. Is this right?

→ Are you worrying that I'm going behind your back?

→ Do you think I was way off with this?

➜ I hear you, and I'm terribly sorry. My actions did not come from bad intentions. Rather, it was in the spirit of keeping things moving without overburdening you with e-mails.

➜ I apologize. I will copy you on any of these communications in the future.

➜ Please accept my apologies. I'm determined to not have this repeat itself and will call you at least once a week to keep you up to date.

➜ I heard your message loud and clear. I'm sorry. I'll make sure it doesn't happen again.

➜ Next time, I'll check with you first before doing anything.

➜ In the future, I'll make it my number one priority to keep you updated each step along the way.

Perfect Phrases for an Applied-Fee Disagreement

Money can be a tough topic with customers. You need to strike a balance between empathizing and standing your ground.

→ What you are saying is that we overcharged you for this service. Correct?

→ I have found the record. You're right that those are the fees that have been applied to you. What do you think is wrong about them?

→ Yes, I see. You are correct that we have applied these fees. Are you disputing them?

→ Do you understand what's behind this number? Has anybody explained to you yet what we had to do?

→ The objective of our fee structure is to have a values-based fee structure. That means the more involved the service, the more it costs. In your situation, for example, we had to _____, _____, and _____.

→ Our goal is to cover our service costs. At the same time, we want happy customers.

→ We want to fulfill your service needs at a price where you feel you are getting a good value.

→ We have an extended warranty program that would have covered these additional charges. Would you like to enroll in that program now for future situations like this?

➜ You are an important customer. Since you didn't know this detail before, we will offer you _____.

➜ We want to have you as a customer for a long time. Therefore, we will waive this fee.

➜ Indeed, our fee structure has changed for all of our customers. Due to increased costs in _____, we have increased fees across the board. This was in the information packet we mailed. Have you received it?

➜ I am sorry to hear the information about the new fee structure did not reach you. To acknowledge this fact, and in appreciation for your loyal business, we are willing to stay with the old fee structure for this last order.

Perfect Phrases for Triangulation: Service and Sales

Sometimes the transition from sales to customer service is challenging both for the sales representative and for the customer. If your customer continues to rely on the salesperson for customer-service issues, you'll need to address this directly.

→ Thank you very much for calling with this question.

→ If I understand you correctly, you have a question about the _____ we delivered to you last week.

→ I very much appreciate our relationship.

→ Have I mentioned to you that you should be calling _____ with this question? Is there a problem with our service that you are calling me?

→ We want to be able to get your issue handled in the best possible way. Were you unable to get your issue handled by Customer Service?

→ Our customer service department does nothing but answer calls like yours. Would you feel comfortable communicating directly with them in the future?

→ As I mentioned earlier, the real experts who can answer this question are my colleagues in Customer Service. May I transfer you?

→ Next time, please talk to _____ in Customer Service. She will be taking care of you going forward.

→ I will be there in the background helping as needed. Going forward, please call _____ for an order issue.

→ This time I will help you. If there are any issues in the future, please call _____.

→ Don't take this the wrong way. My job is to serve you. For day-to-day issues, however, please talk to _____. He and I meet once a month to review your account.

Perfect Phrases for When a Customer Is Unhappy About Customer Service

When a customer calls with a complaint, there is good news and bad news. The bad news, of course, is that something went wrong. However, the good news is the customer is calling. This gives you the opportunity to fix the problem. Remember in these situations to always listen, apologize, and do what you can to make up for the error.

→ If I understand you right, you are calling to complain about the response you have received from Customer Service. We take those issues very seriously. Thank you for calling.

→ Please explain what happened.

→ Have you called us about this matter before?

→ You're right; you shouldn't be spoken to like that.

→ I see. You waited two days for a response and today were put on hold for too long before being connected to me.

→ Do you agree that the objective is to solve your problem in the most expedient way without you having to have to be without your _____?

→ We are trying to get back to each customer within twenty-four hours.

→ Taking everything into consideration, how could we best serve you now?

→ Good, this is what we're going to do: first _____,
   then _____, and finally _____. Do you agree
   with this?

→ I will check in with you again on _____ to make
   sure this has been resolved.

→ Let us make it up to you by _____.

Perfect Phrases When a Mistake Upsets the Customer

The nightmare of any businessperson: You discover your customer is upset and it is your fault. When it is your fault, say so, as soon as possible. Customers are likely to forgive once, with an honest, humble apology. Use these phrases to help create success.

→ I am calling you because I made a big mistake.

→ We had made changes to improve _____. Unfortunately, the changes did not work. In fact, they created a different problem.

→ Our goal is to be the best in industry results. Unfortunately, this time we missed the mark.

→ You know how important a customer you are to us. We would never want to do anything to jeopardize this relationship. I hope you can forgive us for this mistake.

→ My intuition usually serves me very well. In this case, I misjudged the situation.

→ I know that we made a poor decision. I wonder what you think we could do next time to not run into this problem.

→ Please tell me what you have heard on your end.

→ How do you assess the situation?

→ Who else has been impacted?

→ Our goal is 100 percent satisfaction. What can we do to make this up to you?

→ We are committed to ensuring this does not happen again. We are going to _____.

→ As you know, we have provided this service for _____ years. This is the first time this has happened.

→ I know we are partly to blame for this. However, we need your help to fix this. Are you willing to support us?

→ We have several options to address this going forward. There are _____, _____, and _____. Which one works best for you?

→ If you want us to assign a different person on the project next time, I would understand.

→ We are fully committed to this project, now even more than before. We want to prove to you that we can do better and that this is not how we do business.

→ You will see a difference going forward.

→ We are going to ratchet up our oversight to ensure higher performance next time.

→ As a sign of our commitment to you and your company, we are going to offer you _____.

Perfect Phrases for Customer Complaints on Unresponsiveness

Assess the situation. Apologize where necessary, but also assert your point of view. Use these phrases to help calm the conflict.

→ Thank you very much for raising the issue.

→ Please continue to let me know of any problems so I can address them right away.

→ Having no secrets between us is critical. If we can't talk to each other, we will never be able to be productive.

→ Being informed is top priority since more than just the two of us are involved.

→ I will check back in _____ days/weeks to see how it is going.

→ I will bring this to my boss's attention. It is important feedback.

→ Really? I apologize. Tell me more about what happened.

→ This is on the critical path for the project, so let's get it addressed right away. Could you let me know what it looked like from your point of view?

→ We really appreciate our relationship and take your complaint seriously. Let me check what happened and I will get back to you within twenty-four hours.

→ I am looking at your record. It seems the shipment left on time. Let me look into this and see why you didn't receive it.

→ We wouldn't have had the success we've had without your contribution. This seems to be our first glitch. Let's discuss it right away.

→ Thank you for bringing this up. There seems to be a discrepancy between your expectations and how our processes work. Let's schedule a time to discuss this in more detail.

→ This may be a misunderstanding; however, our terms say _____. We are still within this time frame.

→ I apologize for this oversight. How can we make up for it?

→ We pride ourselves on our customer service. However, what you are asking for is way above what we can reasonably do. We can offer you these three options: _____, _____, and _____. Which would you prefer?

→ No, unfortunately, this is not possible. What I can offer you is _____.

→ I am sorry you are so disappointed. Unfortunately, this is the best we can do right now. I am committing for the future to better explain the options. Also, I will let you know ahead of time if there is an expected delay.

→ If you look at our terms and conditions, you will see that we specifically state _____. The reason we do this is _____. I apologize that this is putting you in a difficult spot. Is there anything I can do in the meantime?

Perfect Phrases for Introducing a Price Increase

Price increases are never a pleasant message. Remember, however, that your customers don't buy on price alone. Use these phrases to reduce conflict by addressing the breadth of your offering and how you are contributing to their business.

➜ You will be receiving a letter/e-mail with all the details. Since you are an important customer, however, I wanted to alert you to the fact that we are introducing a price increase. We are increasing _____ by _____.

➜ We have not had a price increase since _____. The reason we are doing it now is _____.

➜ You are right, we did increase our prices last _____. However, in order to address _____, we need to do it again now.

➜ I know you are getting pressure to keep your costs down. This price increase has been instituted . . .

   ➜ to maintain the high level of service you have been receiving.

   ➜ to continue to provide the same level of quality.

   ➜ to keep consistently reliable delivery.

➜ I know this is not a pleasant message. Since we are talking . . .

   ➜ tell me, how are we doing?

→ what are your customer's needs with this product/service?

→ what else can we offer to help you?

→ As you know, we have just received an award for _____. We lead the market in _____. In spite of that, our pricing is very competitive.

→ Would you be willing to increase the volume to _____ to receive a discount and make up for the price difference?

→ We understand your concern. Let me discuss it with my boss. I will get back to you by _____.

→ You brought up some good ideas. I will discuss them internally and get back to you.

Perfect Phrases for a Supplier That Doesn't Follow Through on an Agreement

The best supplier relationships are formed on win/win partnerships. Use these phrases to clearly address the issues. At the same time, work to strengthen the partnership for the future.

→ I really appreciate our relationship. We have had a lot of success together.

→ I am very aware that we wouldn't have had the success we've had without your contribution.

→ It seems like things are not running as smoothly as they have in the past, and I would like to discuss that with you.

→ We selected you based on . . .

  → your references.

  → your presentation and proposal.

  → your promises at the signing of the contract.

→ I was looking forward to working on this project. This seems to be our first glitch and I think we'd best discuss it right away.

→ Last week, we agreed that you were going to . . .

  → process the payment.

  → deliver the drawings.

  → finish the software.

  → fix the error.

  → send the proposal.

- → call _____.
- → pour the foundation.
→ Unfortunately,
  - → it didn't happen.
  - → I didn't get a phone call.
  - → I was alerted of the delay only now.
  - → I learned through a third party that this was not feasible.
→ This is really frustrating.
→ I feel taken advantage of.
→ There may be perfectly good reasons for _____, but without hearing from you I don't know what is happening on your end.
→ This was on the critical path for the project and now everyone is getting nervous about hitting the deadline. In addition, I am getting complaints from the team about being a roadblock. What happened?
→ Could you let me know what it looked like from your point of view?
→ How did we end up here?
→ The way I like to work is that . . .
  - → if there are changes, let me know as soon as you know.
  - → if there is bad news, just tell me.
  - → having no secrets between us is critical. If we can't talk to each other, we will never be able to be productive.
  - → being informed is top priority since there are more than just the two of us involved.

→ What can we do to make sure this doesn't happen in the future?

→ Are you willing to commit to do what we agree to in the future?

→ Will you agree to provide me with early warning of problems?

→ What else can you do to increase my confidence that this will not repeat itself?

→ This is not the first time something has happened. I think we have been tolerant and understanding. Let me be clear. This is the last chance. If you don't fix this problem, we will have to work with another company.

→ I hope you don't mind if I send you an e-mail documenting this discussion.

→ I would like this conversation to be documented. Please send me your commitment by _____.

→ I assume you understand that, in light of the gravity of this situation, we are also expecting _____ to confirm our (new) understanding.

→ By when can I expect your call laying out your corrective measures?

→ I hope you understand this is not personal, but I am on the hot seat. It seems we have gone as far as we can go. Please have your manager call me to address this.

Perfect Phrases for When a Supplier Doesn't Resolve a Problem

You may be upset by your supplier's failure to meet the terms of the contract. Choose the phrases below that help you express your disappointment, investigate why this problem happened, and figure out what needs to be done to prevent similar situations in the future.

→ I appreciate our business relationship. In this situation, however, I am under the impression that you haven't done anything to address our problem.

→ What is going on with _____?

→ What other information do you need from us so that you can resolve _____?

→ We want to create a long-term relationship with your company. Unfortunately, I am beginning to have my doubts since you have been unresponsive with _____.

→ When we first signed an agreement, you had promised _____. This is not happening. Let me tell you what has happened.

→ I would appreciate hearing your perspective. I want to make this work.

→ What do you think is going on?

→ Am I the only one complaining about this situation?

→ Is there anything I should do differently?

→ My strategy is to not bother you unless it is business critical. When I do call, I need to get a sense of urgency from your end.

→ Could I ask you to return any call within twenty-four hours?

→ I would prefer to get a short note or message saying "We are looking into this issue" than to not hear anything for a week.

→ Is there a better person to call to get this resolved?

→ Would you prefer an e-mail or a phone call when similar situations come up?

→ Thank you. I appreciate your responsiveness and courtesy. I trust this is solved.

→ I will call you in a week to confirm.

Perfect Phrases for When a Supplier Takes Advantage of You

When you are a small company in a sea of larger accounts, you may run into the situation of being on the "C" list. The following phrases will help get your issues resolved.

→ I am calling you with an important issue. We bought _____ and took your full service package. After only eighteen months of use, the products are shutting down unexpectedly. This grinds our whole production to a halt.

→ We have been doing business for _____. I know you are growing and taking on larger accounts. The problem is that your service with us is slipping.

→ Please go into your records and check our service history. What do you see?

→ I was just on the phone for three hours with _____. He ended by sending me back to you. We cannot go on like this. What can you do for me?

→ The delays and shutdowns mean lost money from lost production time. We can't meet our orders on time.

→ When we decided to go with your company, our vision was 99.9 percent uptime. Is this something you can live up to?

→ How are we going to get past this?

→ What other ideas do you have to make sure this doesn't happen again?

→ Who else needs to be involved in this discussion to ensure we get this resolved?

→ Would it be possible for you to send someone out here and make sure we are not doing anything wrong?

→ This is unacceptable. Unless this is resolved by _____, we will need to find another supplier.

→ You are not living up to our original agreement. I will have to inform my boss of this situation so we can decide what to do next.

Perfect Phrases for Unethical Behavior by a Supplier or Customer

You do not want to be the headline of your newspaper tomorrow. Use these phrases when you find yourself in an uncomfortable, unethical, or illegal situation with a supplier or customer.

→ I appreciate our relationship. You are a key person for our company and for myself. However . . .

  → this is against our corporate rules about giving gifts.

  → this would break the law.

  → this would give the impression of _____.

  → if this were to become public, it would be embarrassing for me and my company.

→ Instead, why don't we meet for dinner and have some fun.

→ Thank you very much for your generous gift. I sure appreciate it. However, my company does not allow me to accept gifts over _____. I am 100 percent happy with our work relationship. You do not need to send anything in the future.

→ I read those articles in the press/I have been approached by people telling me that your company has . . .

  → unsafe conditions for your workers in _____.

  → children working in your facility.

  → been bribing public officials.

- → been collaborating with other suppliers to set prices.

- → been paying one of our employees to work for you on the side.

- → discriminated against _____ in the hiring process.

→ I have been asked internally to get more information on this from you by tomorrow. I will also have to inform our compliance people, who may approach you separately.

Perfect Phrases for Dealing with a Difficult Supplier Contact

When companies begin to work with a new supplier contact who is abrasive, the problem can easily escalate. Use these phrases to try to work things out directly.

→ Our companies have been working together for a long time. Recently, it has become very difficult.

→ It seems to me like our relationship has not been ideal. Let me give you an example:

- → You take several days to respond to my e-mails.

- → When I call you, I get voice mail and no replies.

- → You respond to questions defensively.

- → It is very difficult to find a mutual time to meet.

- → Meetings have been rescheduled multiple times.

→ You say you are busy, but I know you make time for other customers as you often tell me you are in a customer meeting.

→ When we finally meet, we are interrupted by you checking your messages and answering the phone.

→ I understand that _____. I am not talking about just one case. This same thing has happened _____, and there seems to be a pattern. It is happening so often that we wonder how you view our relationship.

→ How do you see our relationship?

→ How do you define the standards of our relationship?

→ What would you do in our situation?

→ Please feel free to give me your reactions. The expectations that I have are . . .

   → a response time of _____.

   → regular meetings every _____.

   → status reports every _____.

   → the development of a scorecard of criteria of productivity, quality, efficiency, and relationship that we can use to discuss how we are doing.

→ You are right, I am not perfect. I have done _____. I am happy to talk about that, too.

→ I would gladly get together with you and your manager to discuss this.

→ This has been serious enough that I will want to escalate it with your manager. Before I do so, how are we going to resolve this for the future?

Perfect Phrases for a Supplier That Changes Focus

In spite of assurances of business as usual, the dynamics of companies can change as they are acquired or merge. Find out what is happening and address issues by using these phrases.

→ Congratulations. We heard about your merger with XYZ. What does that mean for you personally? What do you expect will change for us?

→ We went to the website and investigated your PR material about the combined company. We may have some potential issues we have to address.

　→ You are now also the supplier for one of our main competitors.

　→ Your new combined company has offerings that compete directly with our products.

　→ You seem to be dealing directly with some of our customers.

　→ We appreciate the personal relationship we have with you. We fear we may have to deal with someone else.

　→ The location of your factory is critical to ensure short delivery times. We hope distances won't increase through the consolidation.

→ Since the merger, we have observed that . . .

　→ you are less available. You seem to be consumed with a lot of travel and meetings. It is difficult to find others in your organization familiar with our needs to help us.

→ we suddenly have multiple points of contact and don't know who to contact for what.

→ we are getting conflicting messages from different people.

→ My objective is to keep the same service level. Specifically, we want to make sure we have . . .

→ one point of contact.

→ better response times.

→ delivery within _____.

→ pricing of _____.

→ I understand that this is a big change and that change is the nature of our world. In this new situation, I would appreciate getting candid information on what is happening.

→ Let's not pretend things are how they used to be. We are happy to adapt, but we need to know early on where you are heading.

→ We are worried. You are important to our business. We need your support and an open exchange of information to make this work during this transition.

→ Let's talk about potential scenarios and our alternatives for responding to them. What do you see coming?

→ I have heard those rumors about your internal processes changing. What is true?

→ What are some of your internal deadlines in your reorganization?

→ By when do you think you will have a consolidated new strategy?

→ Would it make sense to organize a meeting with _____ of both of our companies to discuss some of these issues? Who should we invite?

→ Is there any official communication beyond the general press release you can send me to share with my management?

→ The strength of our collaboration has been our flexibility and our speed. As long as we can keep this up, we are in good shape. Otherwise, we will need to find new solutions.

→ Would your boss be willing to call my boss to discuss _____?

→ Let's create a list together of all the issues we need to address by _____. We can identify who will be in charge of addressing each item.

→ I understand you don't know what you don't know. This is why we should share information frequently. Let's talk every _____.

→ Based on what I understand, our companies are moving in different directions. It seems like we need a way to separate amicably.

→ If these issues cannot be solved to our satisfaction by _____, unfortunately we will have to look for another supplier.

→ I'd like you to know that, based on this new situation, we are soliciting new requests for proposals on your business services. We will invite you to submit and compare you to your competitors.

→ Due to our multiple-supplier policy, since you have merged with our other supplier, we will have to invite a new vendor into the mix.

CHAPTER 6

Perfect Phrases for Conflict with Difficult Personalities

I n this chapter, we introduce you to four difficult personalities and how they respond to conflict. Some people are more aggressive, while others are more passive. The same type of conflict may look distinctively different depending on which personalities are involved. We include sample phrases for each personality type to illustrate the different ways to handle the situation.

People Pleasers

You know the types who will tell you what you want to hear. When you ask them how things are going, they will give a one-word, positive answer such as "OK." Or they may say something like "Thanks for asking. Things are good. Plugging along." Or even "I am sorry this happened. I will take care of it next time," but never follow through.

Why do people pleasers do this? They like to be liked, and, as a result, they are conflict avoiders. They will often go to great lengths to avoid saying "no." Sometimes they have an unrealistic sense of time and the work involved so they promise more than they can deliver.

To handle these types of people during a conflict, first reassure them. They need to understand that saying "no" is not a problem but that not living up to a commitment *is* a problem. Second, help them create realistic estimates of the time and work involved in a project, and then create a compromise based on your needs and their "realistic" resources. The key steps for dealing with people pleasers are:

1. **Make it OK to tell the truth.** Take the time to tell these people that you are interested in their point of view. Reassure them that it is OK if they disagree. Even further, explain that you are looking for their point of view, as you know that you may be wrong.

2. **Be very specific.** If and when you are getting vague or nonspecific answers, ask very specific questions, such as "What do you think we need to do to make this work?" "How long do you think it will take to do step a?" "Based on your years of experience, what problems do you think I could expect?"

3. **Don't put them under pressure.** People pleasers live and die through acceptance. If they don't open up, you may want to give them some time to think and send you an e-mail with their thoughts. If they do take the chance to open up, don't push back too hard. Better to accept a little than push for a lot.

4. **Record agreements.** Writing down agreements is a good idea, mostly for follow-up. The document will provide a basis to

check in and ensure that progress is being made. Also, always end "conflict" conversations with people pleasers by thanking them for their input. Reinforce that you appreciate the two-way dialogue and that their relationship is valued.

Perfect Phrases for Handling a People Pleaser

→ I want to discuss this problem with you. We have to make sure it doesn't happen again.

→ I hear you, that you feel bad. I accept your apology.

→ Whatever the cause is OK with me. I am not here to pass judgment. I just want to make sure the problem is solved and prevented in the future.

→ Let's see what we can do to make sure this doesn't happen again.

→ Could you tell me a little bit of what happened this time, because I don't want to put you in a tough position again next time?

→ What, if anything, did I do that made it hard for you to comply with my request?

→ What, if anything, got in the way of getting this project done on time?

→ What can I do next time to make it easier for you?

→ What, if anything, was particularly challenging?

→ How can we improve our communication so you can give me early warning if you're running into trouble again?

→ Is there any assistance or development you need to make the process smoother next time?

→ I will send you a short e-mail outlining what we agreed on for our records.

Steamrollers

Think of how a steamroller moves forward, with all its weight, to flatten new road pavement. If you get in the way, it will just squash you. The goal is to pave the road, so don't stand in its way.

Some people behave like this during conflict. They want to achieve their goal at all costs. They do whatever needs to get done, including squashing you and your point of view. You know you are dealing with a steamroller if he or she says things like:

- I am very busy and I have very little time for this meeting.

- You are wasting our time. I see what you are doing.

- I think you are completely off base.

- What you are doing doesn't add anything to the business, which is why I don't expect to spend any time with you.

- Don't expect me to change. Look, you are just adding another report where I already have to do the same report for _____. What you are asking me to do is useless.

Steamrollers value strength, so you need to show them you are serious and will stand up for your point of view. You must be

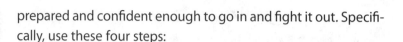

prepared and confident enough to go in and fight it out. Specifically, use these four steps:

1. **Hear him or her out (briefly).** A steamroller wants your respect. He or she has a strong ego and wants to be seen as important, right, and valued. Listen to what a steamroller has to say and try to understand it. If you do this, he or she will be more likely to listen to your point of view.

2. **Break into the conversation.** A steamroller can go on and on as a strategy to wear you down. Take time to listen to the main points, but when he or she starts repeating, be assertive and jump in. He or she expects a debate. If you don't engage, a steamroller will see you as weak. Get his or her attention. Using a firm voice, say something like "All right, I hear you, I hear you," or "Let's see, let's see, let's see." You can even say his or her name repeatedly.

3. **Show the steamroller that you heard him or her.** Demonstrate your respect by repeating back the main points as you heard them. Using the listening skills outlined in Chapter 1, find a way to paraphrase back your understanding of his or her point of view.

4. **Firmly present your point of view.** When you speak to a steamroller, look him or her in the eye. This tells him or her you are confident and are not going to be a pushover. Use a firm, strong tone of voice, but do not try to yell louder than him or her—this will be seen as an attack. Don't fall into the trap of making the steamroller wrong and yourself right. Accept his or her point of view, and offer yours. Now that yours is on the table, you will have to go throught the four phases of conflict resolution to come up with a solution that meets both of your needs.

Perfect Phrases for Handling a Steamroller

Interrupt the steamroller by calling his or her name—repeatedly, if necessary. Once you have his or her attention you say:

→ I'm sorry; I had no idea how deeply I had touched you and that my behavior in the past may have been inappropriate. I apologize for any inconvenience and ill feelings this may have caused for you.

→ Thank you, I appreciate your feedback. Your belief is that I'm not adding value to the discussion. Right?

→ This is feedback I appreciate and I'd be interested to explore further how I could improve in those situations. I value your opinion!

→ It sounds like you think I am not adding any value to the business. What do you mean?

→ You may be doing similar things for _____. However, . . .

> → this report is actually difficult because _____.
>
> → the purpose of this report is _____.
>
> → this report has already helped in a similar situation with _____.
>
> → _____ pays close attention to this report.

→ I didn't realize that. Tell me more about it.

→ I hear you. I see it differently. Where you mention _____, I have observed _____.

→ I don't have any data supporting your comment that _____. On the other hand, there seems to be a lot of data indicating _____.

→ Last month, _____ said _____. This supports my assumption that _____.

→ I would be happy to discuss each of the points you made in detail. My research and analysis led to very interesting results you may not be aware of. When shall we meet?

Attackers

Some people become very aggressive when you approach them with an issue. Maybe they insult you, blame you, or even call you names. Fundamentally, these people do not take responsibility for an issue but rather find a way to make it your fault. This behavior might stem from a pattern of bullying and trying to get their way, or it could be their acting out from a past grievance they have with you.

You will know you are talking to an attacker if you politely bring up an issue, and the attacker goes right for your jugular. You are now on the defensive. They may say something like, "This is not the first time I have heard you come up with a half-baked plan," or "Leave me alone," or even "You know that I'm not the only one who thinks like that, people talk about you."

Whatever the case, to resolve a conflict with an attacker you need to:

1. **Share the impact of the attack.** An attacker needs to know that his or her behavior does not occur in a vacuum and that it

is impacting those around. Be specific, citing examples of what this person did and how you felt, how it impacted the team and others, and how it affected productivity.

2. **Stand your ground.** Once you bring the issue out, an attacker will try to shift the focus to you or others. He or she may even bring up good points. The goal, however, is to keep the focus on his or her attacks and their impact. Keep coming back to citing specifics and their impact to force the attacker to face your feedback.

3. **Listen to the attacker's point of view.** Sometimes you are being attacked because people are upset at you for something you did. Pay close attention to what the attacker is saying. If he or she brings up valid points or concerns, take the time to address them.

4. **Request a change of behavior.** Once it is clear that there is no other reason for the attack than that it is the other person's communication approach, ask if he or she is willing to make a change. Be specific. Ask for what you want him or her to do differently, and remember to reinforce the reason why you are asking for this behavior change. It is not just because you are being a stickler but because there is a negative personal and business impact.

5. **Escalate, if necessary.** For an attacker who is not willing to work with you, you will need to escalate the issue to the appropriate party. You may need your manager to intervene, to mediate, or to give you coaching.

Perfect Phrases for Handling an Attacker

→ I wanted to talk to you about something, which has been bothering me and is interfering with the productivity of our team.

→ Last week you said _____. It's not the first time that I have seen this happen and it makes me feel lousy. I'm getting angry and it dramatically compromises the work of our team.

→ Could we talk about this?

→ Do you understand where I'm coming from?

→ Could you talk about your point of view?

→ I hear you.

→ Could we agree for the future that you very specifically tell me what you need, what you don't understand, or what you don't like rather than attacking me? This will allow me to learn and better accommodate your point of view.

→ I want to be able to hear your suggestions and have a dialogue with you. However, when I hear you bashing me as a person, it's hard for me to concentrate on what you are saying. It just plain hurts.

→ I see things differently. I appreciate your point of view and will incorporate it as I move forward. But my assumptions were _____.

→ Your point _____ is very well taken. I will implement it immediately. Thank you for bringing it up.

→ What I'm here to discuss with you is that I don't want to be ignored anymore. On the other hand, I'm also willing to accommodate your needs and be more responsive.

→ I need your collaboration and your time when the project calls for it. Instead, I am getting attacked for not including you at the end of the process. This is not working.

→ I have tried to work it out with you and am very willing to put more effort into it

→ In the future, in a similar situation, I would appreciate it if we can take the time to talk about this early in the process before emotions build up and our conversation turns into a "he said, she said" kind of thing.

→ How do you think we could make this happen?

→ For the time being, you seem to be shutting the door.

→ I have to think about what I do next. But in the meantime, I want to assure you that my door is wide open and that I'm sorry that we have to end this conversation this way.

→ Since we can't agree, I have to escalate this to my manager. Let's think this through for a moment before I do. Can we reconnect tomorrow morning?

→ I want to close the conversation on a positive note. What am I overlooking? Are there other possibilities?

Emotional Land Mines

Some people have a pattern of exploding unexpectedly. It is like stepping on a land mine that you didn't know was buried there. For example, you are having what seems like a regular conversation, and, all of a sudden, your colleague starts yelling or crying.

Of course, everyone gets emotional at times. However, for some, this emotionality builds up and explodes. Others then avoid approaching them for fear of upsetting them.

Here are four steps to handle an emotional land mine without getting a limb blown off:

1. **Give the person space to explode.** You will encounter emotional land mines, whether you like it or not. Don't try to control the other person.

2. **Ask how he or she would like to proceed.** When you hit an emotional land mine, not only are you taken off guard, but the person who explodes is as well. He or she may be embarrassed by the intensity of the reaction. Often the best strategy is to ask if he or she wants to discuss it further right away or to take a break and come back to this discussion later. He or she—or even you—may need to collect him- or herself before being able to have a productive conversation.

3. **(later) Check in.** Once the other person is ready to continue the conversation, explore whether anything you said upset him or her, whether it was the topic, or whether it was unrelated. You want to give the other person an opportunity to save face by explaining what happened so he or she doesn't feel guilty about being overly emotional.

4. **Get back to the point at hand.**

Perfect Phrases for Handling an Emotional Land Mine

→ I recognize you have a lot of strong feelings about this. I am not sure whether you want to hear an answer from me or discuss this further now or whether you'd rather take a break and talk about it later.

→ I hear you, that you feel bad. I accept your apology. What can we learn from it?

→ What, if anything, triggered your reaction?

→ Could you tell me what was happening within you at this time?

→ What, if anything, did I do to provoke this reaction?

→ How could I assist you better so we avoid this happening again?

→ What can I do next time to make it easier for you?

→ What, if anything, was particularly challenging in this situation that may have contributed to this reaction?

→ Have you had this same pattern with other people also? How have they reacted and how did you solve the problem then?

→ If you think the meeting is not good timing, you will let me know at the beginning.

→ You will look at me and make eye contact before you start talking to better coordinate.

→ We will get together briefly to prepare for the meeting.

→ We will highlight critical topics in an e-mail before the meeting.

→ We will clearly assign topics between the two of us and each of us will take the lead accordingly.

→ We will wait to address emotional topics until after the meeting.

→ Now that we worked that out, let's get back to the main issue we were discussing.

About the Authors

Over the past twenty years, Lawrence Polsky and Antoine Gerschel have lived strategy implementation challenges in many shapes and forms in the United States, Europe, and Asia. They have more than fifteen years of experience developing award-winning programs that improve business communication and leadership within global, multicultural settings.

Antoine's senior management experience enables him to consult, coach, and train leaders with a practical business approach. An extraordinary executive coach, Antoine approaches human problems with a powerful mix of business perspective and sensitivity to human factors.

Lawrence is a business-minded learning and development specialist with the ability to quickly analyze business situations and design learning scenarios and events, which have energized audiences of all sizes and makeups. He is an entrepreneur who, after a career in the financial services, health-care, and consumer-electronics industries, launched and managed two successful businesses. He has also built a gourmet organic food-service business and then an OD & training business.

The authors are founding partners at PeopleNRG, Inc. (www .peoplenrg.com), in Princeton, New Jersey. With speeches, workshops, and coaching assignments, they inspire leaders around the world to propel their teams, divisions, or companies in new directions.

Offerings from PeopleNRG include:

- facilitation of business conflicts, such as subsidiary and HQ alignment issues, postmerger/postacquisition integration, and conflicts within teams and between executives
- keynotes
- executive coaching
- workshops and webinars
- change management programs
- team-building events
- leadership development programs
- leader and team assessments
- engagement metrics